God's House! Beautiful! Let's Go!

Jane Ann Derr

with an Afterword by
STEPHEN BROYLES

xulon
PRESS

The Anchor of the Soul

Loved ones come and loved ones go;
The Word of God abides forever.
Friends come and friends go;
The Word of God lives forever.
Happiness comes and happiness goes;
The Word of God delights forever.
Success comes and success goes;
The Word of God challenges forever.
Fortunes come and fortunes go;
The Word of God provides forever.
Houses come and houses go;
The Word of God stands forever.
Good health comes and good health goes;
The Word of God endures forever.
Memories come and memories fade;
The Word of God lasts forever.
The seasons come and the seasons go;
The Word of God is forever.
Earth and heaven shall vanish away;
The Word of God shall remain forever.

J.A.D.

Contents

Preface

Jesus Christ is the same yesterday and today and forever.

—Hebrews 13:8 (NKJV)

My dear husband, Harold, passed away September 18, 2006. My life's companion, my dearest friend, my protector was gone. After the funeral was over, after the family and friends had gone, after the reality of my great loss had began to sink in, I felt the need to record these events in my journal, before the memories faded like the outgoing tide and were lost to sight. My journals gave me a place to file away my feelings until I was able to deal with them and then release them to God.

I had Harold's papers to go through—his writings and sermons and recordings. I found television sermons that Harold preached twenty-five years ago. He frequently addressed the subject of death. In one of his sermons, "How Will You Die?" his theme was that *how you die depends on how you have lived.*

We will all one day walk through the valley of the shadow of death, and we will find God's help even there. Just as the angels helped Jesus the Christ in his passage, they will help us. And yet Jesus still had to walk that valley. He spent agonizing hours in prayer for the strength to go through his trials and death on the cross. That reminds us that we too need to prepare, diligently and prayerfully, for the eventual destiny of all mankind. Our strength from God comes when we seek his help and guidance regularly before the emergency happens. Then we can think clearly without becoming confused. We can open our eyes and see God working in all things. We can operate then with the confidence of a well trained fireman putting out a fire.

Harold loved plants and filled the sunroom of our home with lush plants of all kinds—especially peace lilies. He cared for them every day. Now that Harold is gone, I have had to learn how to keep these beautiful plants alive and looking their best. I've discovered that part of this daily process is to prune away the dead leaves. No matter the age of the plants—young or old—they all need pruning to keep them at their best. Part of the preparation for writing this book has been to understand that pruning is a life-long process.

In time I came to feel a deep desire that God had put on my heart to write this book and inspire readers to see the tremendous strength, guidance, and overwhelming love of God as it is revealed in his Word and in the experiences of our lives. Like a father who wants to protect, guide, and help his children, God wants to help us.

God will be with us in this present moment, in death, and in Heaven. "Jesus Christ is the same yesterday and today and forever" (Heb. 13:8 NKJV).

Part One of this book contains narratives about our lives and often draws upon my journals. These tell how God proved to me that the Bible is a living book and that we can safely rest on God's promises. Part Two contains some of the resources that helped me along the way. Especially in my prayer journals I found strength in seeing how God answered prayer and sent help to comfort in our trials and times of need. God wants us to be his daily friend and tell him our daily needs. He is just waiting to whisper a new blessing into our listening ear as he guides us to find it. "I bless the holy name of God with all my heart. Yes, I will bless the Lord and not forget the glorious things he does for me" (Ps. 103:1 TLB).

I have here and there mentioned my promise to Harold to complete a book about our family's missionary work in Africa. That book has been published as *Trailblazing With God: Learning To Walk on the Water* (Longwood, Florida: Xulon Press, 2008).

I could never have written this book without the help of people who were for me messengers of God and angels of light. When I was bewildered, they covered me with encouragement. When the words got stuck in my throat, they had patience and pulled out my innermost hidden thoughts. When I was stubborn and proud, they gently led me to face myself. When I was wrong, they lovingly forgave me. I owe them my thanks.

Stephen E. Broyles, my faithful, patient editor, who brought order out of my chaotic, rambling thoughts. God surely sent him to help me.

Debbie, Kevin, Diana, Janice, Tim, Cathy, and John, my wonderful children, who never tired of hearing of my struggles with the writing of this book.

John, my patient son, who gave me the gift of his time and listening to me.

Janice and Tim, my daughter and son-in-law, and my daughter Diana, who helped with the editing.

Grace Chapel Church, where every member is a minister. Only God knows how much I have appreciated you for the encouragement you gave me as I faced Harold's illness and death and my own grieving process, for your care for me when I fell, and for your prayers as I agonized with the writing of this book.

Etowah River Church. Your love, prayers, visits, encouragement, and loyalty were a pillar of strength.

Jim, Randy, and John Carroll and the staff at Carroll and Company. I will never forget your kindness and concern for me. Your encouragement greatly influenced the completion of this book.

Dr. Neil R. Lightfoot. Thank you for introducing me to Stephen Broyles and for your kind encouraging words over the years.

Judy Miller. Thank you for your prayers, for our wonderful telephone conversations, and for allowing me to use quotations from your book, *The Last Mile of the Way.*

Dr. Jerry Jones. Thank you for your kind and encouraging words, and for graciously allowing me to use quotations from your book, *Beyond the Storm.*

Bill Long. Thank you for your great example and for allowing me to quote from your personal journals when Laura passed away.

Fern Hill. Thank you for graciously allowing me to use quotations from your book, *Graduation to Glory.*

Amanda Gallegos, our granddaughter. Thank you for your willingness to face your own terrible grief and write the story of the death of your twins.

Thanks to the many other friends and loved ones who prayed and encouraged me.

Thanksgiving, honor, and glory to the Ruler of the Universe: God our Father, Jesus the Christ his Son, and the Holy Spirit, who gave divine guidance in all of the dark moments.

God's House! Beautiful!
Let's Go!

Part 1

Chapter 1
Unexpected Journeys

In his heart a man plans his course, but the Lord
determines his steps.

—Proverbs 16:9

Have you ever tried to complete a project, and
dozens of unexpected hindrances came crashing
down trying to destroy all your efforts? That is how
my husband Harold and I felt in the spring when he
fell and we began the hardest journey of our lives.

Harold was the preacher at a small church of
about fifty to seventy-five people nestled in the
foothills of Georgia's Blue Ridge Mountains, part of
the ancient Appalachian chain.

Local historian Charlene Terrell tells of ancient
tribes before the Creeks and Cherokees, as well as
the pioneers who moved here in the 1830s. The
pioneers were "curious, cautious and clannish stock:
dour, silent Scots; whiskey-drinking, fighting Irish,
proud stubborn English; brooding, secretive Welsh;
fiery French Huguenots and mixed blood Cherokees.
Here, they raised corn, livestock, vegetables and
children. Most also made moonshine whiskey, their

only cash crop" (*Wolfscratch Wilderness* (Roswell, Georgia: W. H. Wolfe, 1994), p. ii).

When we arrived at the church it consisted of three families meeting in a small, termite-infested house on a busy highway. Whenever we pulled into the driveway, we usually had to wait while one of the neighbor's roosters crossed our path. One of the men had tried to repair the furnace. It exploded and he was burned badly. Because of the many challenges, we had become a closely-knit church family.

Weeks turned to months, and months turned to years. God sent willing people who gave their time, finances, and love. Seven and one-half acres of land became available on Etowah River Road in Dawson County. The plot was ideal for a church building at the top of a beautiful hill where horses and sheep had grazed. After the purchase, however, we learned that the deeded right-of-way existed on paper only. The next-door neighbor had put a chain across the road. We had purchased a land-locked plot of ground. We gathered often for seasons of prayer.

At just the right time, God made available three and one-half acres adjoining the original acres with a 280-foot frontage on Etowah River Road. The family who owned the property agreed to sell. At the final signing of this transaction, Harold sat next to the woman who owned the property. She said this piece of ground had been in her family for over 150 years. She cried and said that she didn't want to sell, but she had a strong feeling inside that God wanted her to do this. She cried and signed.

The purchase gave us a right-of-way, but now there was another problem. The land was separated by a mountain stream—Palmer Creek. After the final papers were signed for the three and one-half acres, Harold and I made the difficult climb to the top of the mountain, pushing back the overgrown shrubs blocking our way. I found a large boulder and sat down to rest. Harold stood on the highest ground gazing into the valley below.

"Sweetheart, come here," he said and motioned for me to come. "It will take your breath away."

He lifted me up to where he was standing.

"See!"

He pointed. I looked around and saw a galloping white horse and timid sheep grazing on the velvet pasture lined with emerald-green trees. The brilliant blue sky was a perfect backdrop for the white puffy clouds passing slowly overhead.

"See!" he pointed again. "Can't you just see an old-timey covered bridge over that creek?" His eyes flashed with excitement. "Let's call the bridge Grace." He was silent a few minutes. "It will be called Grace—the bridge from God to man."

I studied his countenance and could see that he was dreaming again.

"I know that this spot is where God wants the church building to be. I can see now a beautiful white Normandy church building with a large, welcoming front porch and—" He paused. "Can't you just imagine what could be done here? A school maybe? A wedding chapel? A retreat? Or a place where Spanish-speaking people can learn English?

God just meant for us to have this land. You know that don't you?"

His voice trailed off as he continued to gaze.

"Yes, sweetheart," I answered softly.

Weeks, months, and years whirled by with many emotional highs and lows. Then it had been eleven years. The bridge had been built, and the church on the hill, and a fellowship building—all except the porch roof.

In our private times together, Harold talked much about how God had blessed him by sending him to Etowah River. He had endured much pain in his childhood town of Blackhawk, Indiana. He had been labeled a half-breed Indian and son of a blacksmith, and his classmates had shunned him. At Etowah River Harold loved the land and animals and appreciated the Indian culture. He had made friends with the people in town. Many had generously donated their labors of love that made the completion of the projects possible.

Harold thanked God many times for allowing the son of a blacksmith to preach the gospel globally, to be a part of the research team that built the Atlas and Thor missiles that sent the first man to the moon, to enjoy the beauty surrounding Etowah River, and to be a part of all of the building projects. He would always say, "Truly God is good to me."

By 2004 I began praying that the women of the church could put together an area-wide women's retreat for the following spring. However this would require the use of the unfinished fellowship building. The floors needed tile, the kitchen needed cabinets, and the entrance porch needed a roof. Harold quickly agreed to work harder to get all of the construction completed. Alone and with blisters on his knees, Harold set about laying the floor tile. We lived twenty miles from the church property. Harold left early every morning in his white 1976 Chevy panel tool truck that he had named Bertha. Every day he loaded all the daily materials and tools he needed to finish each task. Although he enjoyed preaching and teaching, he enjoyed building projects even more. He always found something else to build—a room, a bookshelf, a lamp, or a piece of furniture. He was delighted to continue the construction projects.

After several planning sessions, the retreat was becoming a reality. Women volunteered to help in many areas, and everyone agreed to publish our own cookbook to distribute to our guests. Men and women eagerly contributed their favorite recipes, and the cookbook, *A Taste of Joy*, was completed.

One day as I left the accounting office where I worked, I was caught in a sudden severe thunder storm. I sat in the parking lot. The rain pounded the roof of the car as the wind rocked the car like a boat in a storm. I jumped when lightning struck nearby and could feel my heart race. Time seemed to stall as I waited for the storm to pass. Finally the storm subsided, and I peered through the steamed windshield trying to see the road as the car and I limped home.

As soon as I pulled into our driveway, I sensed something was wrong. Harold's truck was in the driveway instead of his usual spot at the back of the house. I quickly clicked the garage door opener and rushed inside the house. The lights were on. As I walked through the hallway, I glanced into the living room. I was stunned at what I saw. Harold sat limply on the couch. His face was gray and troubled and showed nothing of its usual vibrant, sunny disposition. His body was frail and weak, as if his normally strong and vigorous physical appearance had been wiped away.

"What happened!" I cried.

I rushed to the couch to examine him. I saw a big bump on his head and a bloody gash on his arm.

"We need to get you to the emergency room right away," I said. "What happened?"

"I fell up at the church property." His voice was weak.

"Was someone there to help you?" I probed for answers.

"No," he replied softly. "I was up on a ladder attaching the porch roof to the building and all of a sudden I was on the ground. I just lay there for a few minutes stunned. Then I carefully moved my arms and legs and decided to load up my tools and drive home."

"How far did you fall?"

"Oh, I guess it was about five or six feet. My left arm and shoulder hurt, but I was able to drive home."

As we pulled away in the car on our way to the hospital I noticed that the rain had subsided. We were silent as I drove. Harold always liked to drive and I could feel his anxiety building as I carefully turned into the hospital driveway. I parked in front of the emergency room entrance, and he told me that he was able to get out alone. He told me to park the car and that he would meet me in the waiting room.

As soon as we completed the admission process, the kind nurses directed us to the examining room. Harold was X-rayed and bandaged, and we were told that he had broken ribs, a badly bruised shoulder, a sprained wrist, and a gash on his head. The nurses started injections to ease his pain.

Seven hours later we were able to go home. The rain had now turned into a fine mist. I peered through the steamed windshield into the darkness. Harold was silent. I prayed until we approached our driveway.

Our daughter Diana, who lived nearby, ran out to meet us, along with her grandson, Nathan, and children Amanda and Katherine. Our son John, who lived in New York, had happened to call Harold on his cell phone as he drove home after his fall. When John could not reach us later, he had become alarmed and had called our family from coast to coast. They had begun chain prayers for us, and Diana and her family had come to our house to wait. We spent the next several hours explaining about the accident and praising God for his help in time of need.

All of this happened right before the retreat. The next few days were a whirlwind of activity. Our daughter Janice flew in from Denver, Colorado, to help me with the last-minute details. Diana dropped by after work to help. On Friday afternoon Janice,

Diana, and I went to the church to do some last-minute decorating. Harold remained at home, resting in his comfortable recliner. When we finished at the church, we stopped at a nearby restaurant to take home our evening meal and drove home confident that everything was in proper order.

Diana's car was in the shop being repaired, and Harold had loaned her his restored 1973 Ford Mustang with the 351 Cleveland engine and the high-performance carburetor. This was Harold's pride and joy. It had taken many years for Harold to rebuild this car. It still had the original gas gauge in it—which didn't work properly. When the gas tank was completely full, it registered three-quarters. So it took a lot of concentration to remember how much gas was really in the tank.

When Diana left our house that night, she misjudged the gas gauge. She stopped at the first traffic signal, and suddenly she heard the car choke. She eyed the gas station on the other side of the road. It was just past the light, and Diana felt sure that she could get there with the remaining gas. When the light changed to green, she slowly turned right and began to edge into the center lane to turn left into the station.

Before she reached the turn lane, the Mustang choked again, shook, and died. Diana was in the middle of a heavily traveled highway. It was dark. She was scared. She fished through her purse and finally found her cell phone and called Janice. Janice and I immediately had a short prayer, got into our car, and headed out to help.

Meanwhile Diana sat in the middle of the highway looking around. Although it was a main highway, on this particular night the normally heavy traffic had diminished. Diana's heart pounded. She said a silent prayer. She looked up and saw a car come barreling around the curve and down the hill toward her. She prayed. Each time she saw a car, she pumped the brakes, hoping they would see her stalled on the highway.

When Janice and I reached her, we hardly knew how we could help her without becoming a traffic hazard ourselves. Janice told me to place our car right behind the disabled Mustang. She told me to stay in the car and put on my hazard lights. She jumped out to help Diana push the car into the gas station.

I sat and prayed as Janice and Diana began to push the car. I could feel my heart pounding like a drum. Although it was quite warm, chills penetrated my body. I tried looking at the girls in their bold attempts, but mostly my eyes were closed praying.

When I looked again, they had got the car to the center turning lane. Traffic began to build up, and they waited. I prayed. When a break finally came, the girls pushed the Mustang across the highway into the downhill entrance of the gas station. Suddenly the girls lost control as the car gained speed and began veering toward the pizza restaurant next door.

Diana tried to jump into the driver's seat. She missed! Instead she ended up with one foot in the car, one foot outside, and her rear end dragging the ground. Janice immediately pulled her from the car.

Then I watched stunned as Janice made her own attempt to jump into the car. She also missed!

Now the unmanned Mustang picked up more speed and veered again, this time in the direction of the gas station building. It seemed impossible to stop the car before the destined collision. Suddenly a customer darted out of the gas station. He realized that the runaway Mustang was headed toward his car and the building. He stopped, planted his feet firmly on the ground, and braced himself with outstretched arms like Superman. As the Mustang moved closer, however, the man realized he was not Superman. He rushed to the side of the car, jumped in, and brought it to a halt moments before the car would have collided with the building.

As I looked on the bizarre scene, I heard a round of applause. The patrons at the fuel pumps clapped their hands and laughed. We undoubtedly had been the entertainment of the evening. We were just glad that God had sent an angel in the form of a wannabe Superman who saved Harold's prized Mustang. The girls and I exhaled a giant breath of relief and fervently thanked God for his great blessings to us.

In spite of the previous day's drama, the women's retreat turned out a success. Fifty or sixty women attended. There were classes, a keynote speaker, and a sixteen-member singing group. We laughed. We cried. We enjoyed fellowship and a beautifully prepared meal. We distributed the cookbooks, and we made DVDs and CDs of the day's events so we could enjoy them again later.

Soon after the great uplift that I felt after the women's retreat, a new cloud descended suddenly over my soul. This new cloud engulfed me with a feeling of apprehensive bewilderment. I started becoming aware that Harold's sunny disposition had turned to a dark cloud of solemn silence. I could see that Harold was not recovering from his fall. He frequently looked tired, frail, and discouraged. In all his prayers, public and at home, he prayed, "God, when my work is done, quickly take me home."

Harold started having problems with his eyes. After being examined by the doctor, he was told that his diabetes was causing his eye problems and that it was unwise for him to drive at night or in the rain. We evaluated the situation. I felt very uncomfortable driving the narrow winding mountain roads, especially at night. So we had come to a fork in the road, and we had never traveled this road before. We were in a quandary as we pondered our choices and what the outcome of our choices might be.

Harold's prayer kept bouncing around in my mind, and I wondered what it meant—"When my work is over, quickly take me home." Other thoughts rolled in like unwanted tidal waves. I remembered the mini-stroke that he had suffered the previous year. I remembered my burning anger when he had retreated into silence and I felt he was hiding something from me. I felt like a heavy boulder had crushed me. Something terrible had been wrong and he would not tell me. I remembered something he had told me in one of our tender moments. He had said, "I always told John that big boys don't cry.

That's wrong! I shouldn't have told him that!" He had said this passionately.

At other times I became very angry. We were so looking forward to our special time together when all the church projects were completed so we could be together, just us. Now I sensed that it would never happen.

I cried and prayed and tried bargaining with God. But down deep I knew. So I decided not to waste a second on tears of regret, but to savor every second of the now that was left. So I cried and prayed in private, but maintained a sunny disposition when I was with Harold.

In the end we decided that God was pointing us to the road of retirement from the life at Etowah River. We would announce our decision to the church in May and leave at the beginning of September. We would miss our church family at Etowah River as we started our new journey. We would be attending another church nearby, where we would sit together in the pew and listen.

In July the children worked endlessly planning a party for Harold's seventy-fifth birthday. I sensed that it had begun to register in their minds that their beloved Daddy's health was failing.

All of our children were able to come, as well as some of the grandchildren and great-grandchildren. Our daughter Debbie came from North Carolina with her husband, Kevin, their daughter, Tara, her husband, Shane, and their five-year-old son, Bailey. Our daughter Cathy and her two daughters, Helene and Rachelle, came from Tennessee. Our daughter

Janice and her husband, Tim, came from Colorado. Our daughter Diana, who lived nearby, came with her grandson, Nathan, and her daughters, Amanda and Katherine, and her daughter, Shauna, and her husband, Jeremy, and their daughter, Natalia. Our son John came from New York.

Tim, Kevin, and John helped Harold clear the land around our property. We heard the swooshing of falling trees as the men worked in the yard. I saw Tim on the ladder while Kevin held it. John carried away the limbs. Harold and John loaded the red pickup truck to take the limbs away. The girls kept the prayers going while sitting on the front porch in the swing and in chairs. They called themselves the Gatorade Express Team as they filled glasses and took them to the men.

After living in thirty-two houses in the span of fifty or more years, we savored each moment of living in the home that God had blessed us with. It was spread out enough to handle our large growing family. The grandchildren enjoyed the spacious wooded lot fenced in by tall Leyland cypresses that Harold had planted years before. The house was nestled in the woods at the back of the lot. The secluded, serene atmosphere always calmed our restless spirits at day's end. We felt that God had given us this house for a special purpose, and we thanked God for it every time we drove into the driveway.

The week of the party was tumultuous. Altered plans. Ringing cell phones. New York business conference calls. Memphis business conference calls.

Denver business conference calls. Children laughing. Four bathrooms all full. Hugs and tears.

Cathy and Janice ate the Swiss cheese that Debbie and I had planned to use in Chicken Queen Elizabeth. Debbie was busily cleaning up the kitchen dishes and threw away the chicken broth that Janice and I planned to use for a nice potato leek soup.

We went to Lake Lanier Islands for boat rides. It took several cars to accommodate us. Amid the confusion, the car that Debbie and I were in lost the other cars on the way to the Lake Lanier parking lot. We got out of our car and walked over to an outdoor café on the dock. We found a table, sat down, and looked around. We could not see even one familiar face.

Debbie said, "I'll just call someone on their cell phone in one of the other cars."

My cell phone rang. It was Debbie! We both doubled over laughing. Shortly after, the others found us.

The big event of our week finally came. Everyone blended their talents to make it special. The children prepared the meal: roast turkey breast, dressing, corn pudding, four-bean salad, slaw, homemade sour cream bread, butter, birthday cake, ice cream, and iced tea. Rachelle insisted on making the birthday cake. Although it was her very first cake, it was delicious and beautiful in every way. The other granddaughters helped decorate the house, wrap the gifts, and plan the big presentation of their gifts.

After the meal, we assembled in the sunroom to present the cake and gifts. Kevin was designated to bring in the cake, and Harold worked hard to blow out all of the candles. Cathy started the procession of bringing in the gifts. She led everyone in singing "Kum Bah Yah." Our family had sung this song many times in front of many churches as we had raised funds to go to Ghana, West Africa, in the 1960s. I thought of the words, "Lord, come by here," and my eyes filled with tears. This had been our family theme song, along with "My God and I."

The gifts were presented one at a time and the great-grandchildren helped Harold unwrap each gift. At the conclusion the children insisted that Harold give a speech. He sat back silent for a moment and then boldly said that he was very proud of all of them. He loved them all dearly and deeply respected the uniqueness of each one. He said they were all special snowflakes given to us by God to enrich our lives. He said that he was thankful to God for each of them and for their families. He said that they had all worked together as a team to put this entire week together, and it reminded him of a beautiful snow-covered tree in the wintertime in all of its splendor. All of the snowflakes blended together to form a beautiful sight.

The event ended when Jeremy insisted on taking a family portrait. He had purchased a camera just for the event. He worked hard to get the perfect picture, using the timing device on the camera so he could also be in the picture. Our family's journeys had brought us together into this one portrait. We did not know that another journey had already begun.

The dreaded end of August came. It was now time to step away from the church we had served for twelve years. After Harold's last sermon was preached, one of the leaders asked me to come to the front of the congregation. After a short speech, they unveiled a beautifully framed picture of the bridge called Grace. The congregation had signed words of encouragement and love on the beautiful matting bordering the frame. The tearful orator was stunned and silent. I stumbled through words of thanksgiving for their loving memorial gift.

The retirement party had ended. The sky was turning bright orange as the sun slowly began its journey toward the sunset. I sat in the car waiting for Harold to come. He had lingered long, talking to the people in the church. I sat daydreaming. I was abruptly interrupted when Harold opened the car door and asked me to come with him to the top of the mountain to view the sunset. We stood together. Harold put his arm around me and pointed.

"See!" he exclaimed. "Look at the bridge!"

I snuggled closer and gazed silently at the orange hues of the fading sun reflected from the bridge below.

Chapter 2
The Approaching Storm

Be of good courage, and He shall strengthen your heart, all you who hope in the Lord.
—Psalm 31:24 (NKJV)

As the days and months passed quickly by, we fumbled through settling into our new challenges: adjusting to more free time, going to a new church, renewing past friendships, planning a new daily schedule, and doing long-forgotten maintenance to our house.

Thanksgiving was soon over. The children had all been able to come. We had enjoyable visits. But Janice pulled me aside to voice concern over her Daddy's failing health. This conversation jarred me, because I had until then refused to think about it. Now like a pesky gnat flying around my face that wouldn't leave, this thought kept invading my mind.

As I walked down our driveway toward the road to the mailbox, I watched Harold raking leaves. He carefully put them in the trailer behind the riding mower. It was hard for me to admit how slowly he moved. I thought how different our life had become after that August day as we faced the sunset together looking at the bridge. How I needed that grace now!

I glanced at the stately Leyland cypress trees that lined the long driveway. I was suddenly aware that they were as high as the rooftop. It seemed only days since Harold had planted 150 twelve-inch twigs. Now they were all stately trees. Again I remembered his prayer, "When my work is done, quickly take me home."

Early in December Harold went to his doctor for pain. He was prescribed a medication and told to come back in a month. On December 7, his pain became excruciating. He was treated at the emergency room and told to see his primary care doctor. We tried fervently to get an appointment, but could not. On December 11, we went back to the emergency room. The kind doctor on duty would not let us go until he had probed the cause of Harold's pain. Harold's bladder function had completely shut down, and a urologist surgically installed a catheter. After extensive tests, the doctor came back and said to Harold, "Your prostate cancer has come back."

We were stunned. We did not know he had ever had cancer!

The doctor showed us the test results. There was cancer in the prostate, lower intestine, bowels, and spleen. This was especially shocking, because at periodic check-ups through the years, primary care doctors had never mentioned any problems in these areas.

After this visit we tried continually to find a doctor who would see Harold, and no one would schedule a time. On December 18, he experienced more excruciating pain, and I took him back to the emergency room. This time it was acid reflux. He was given a pain injection and sent home. On

December 19 I tried frantically to get a doctor's appointment, but to no avail.

A couple from church, Kevin and Betty, insisted on driving us to Northside Hospital in Atlanta. We arrived at 1:30 in the afternoon. The hospital gave Harold a pain injection, reviewed his record, and admitted him into the hospital. Kevin, Betty, and I left at eight that evening and drove the thirty-five miles home.

Next day, Bernie from church drove me back to the hospital. When I inquired at the admissions desk, I was told that Harold had been transferred to the oncology floor and the receptionist gave me Harold's room number. When I peeked in his room, Harold welcomed me with a smile. He said that Shauna, our granddaughter, had visited with him a couple of hours last night. She is a registered nurse and worked in the emergency room at that hospital. He then told me that his night nurse in the emergency room had been Heather, Shauna's friend. Heather and her three boys had spent last Thanksgiving with our family. I could tell by Harold's countenance that their presence had helped to bring him joy amidst his pain.

After we briefly exchanged a few words, a doctor came into the room. She announced that she had scheduled further tests including a CT-scan and MRI so they could better diagnose what was causing the pain. Almost immediately, Harold was rolled down the hall in a wheel chair on his way to radiology.

After he was settled in his bed again, I could see the painful expression on his face. A nurse came in shortly, gave him a pain injection, turned on the television, and suggested that he listen to the music channel.

I sat in the chair beside his bed, observing his face and the television screen. Beautiful serene scenes of nature appeared across the screen as the sounds of soft, gentle melodies floated through the air, sounds that reminded me of the rhythmic ocean tide lapping the seashore at sunset and then rushing out to sea, taking the pain away. Shortly Harold became more relaxed, and the painful expression on his face disappeared.

When I glanced at my watch, I realized that it was almost time to meet Bernie downstairs so she could drive me home. I stood by Harold's bed, gently kissed his forehead, and told him that I would be back tomorrow.

At home that night I wrote in my journal.

Tuesday, December 20, 2005. Bernie took me to the hospital again. I stayed all day and she picked me up again at six to take me home. Harold had extensive tests today. He has a nice private room with a bath. He is very near the nurse's station. While they were giving him an MRI and CT-scan, I decided to go downstairs to the hospital cafeteria and buy lunch. With my purse hanging on my arm, I put a huge plate of sweet-and-sour chicken and rice on my tray and tried to manipulate the tray as I poured a glass of iced tea. The next thing I knew, I had sweet-and-sour chicken and rice inside my purse. I had forgotten to zip it. The iced tea spilled all over the floor. I took a deep breath, cleaned up the mess, and went back to Harold's room.

When he came back from radiology, he was in great pain. The nurse gave him a pain injection and turned on the music channel. In the Bible, David played the harp for Saul, and Saul felt better. My curiosity is aroused. I want to research this further.

Wednesday, December 21, 2005. The weather remains good. It is cold but no ice or snow. I slept until 6:30 and woke thinking I heard Harold calling me to get up. I ate breakfast and got ready to go to the hospital again. Bernie came at eight. When I got to the hospital, Harold told me that when he woke up, he found a pill on the bed and took it.

"That was stupid," he told the nurse. "I don't know why I took it not knowing what it was."

The nurse apologized for the pill being in his bed and reassured him that they would find out what it was and take care of any side-effects. The nurse then took his blood pressure and temperature and tested his sugar levels. She finally identified the pill as medication for his blood sugar.

The doctors will do a biopsy of the lymph glands today. They think it is lymphoma and other cancer. They keep doing blood-sugar tests and blood-clotting tests. Harold is taking Plavix, and they can't do a biopsy unless the test comes back fifteen minutes. His test was eleven minutes. This was outside the acceptable limit, so the biopsy cannot be done until later.

I have sent out emails asking for prayers, and many I'm-praying-for-you calls and emails are coming back daily. Last night I gave Harold the book *Healing and Prayer* to read. Bernie and I have had some enjoyable visits. She is so sweet. The doctor hadn't come in to see Harold by two. Our daughter Janice flew in from Denver and came directly to the hospital. Since I was so tired, Janice insisted that I go home to rest. So I called Bernie and she drove me home.

I got a call from Janice at seven this evening. The doctor had come in and said that it was cancer of the lymph glands: non-Hodgkin diffuse large B-cell lymphoma, probably stage III or IV. The oncologist said they would be able to do a biopsy Thursday, because by that time the blood-clotting tests would probably be within the acceptable limits. John, our son, was in Charlotte at nine, so he will be home in four hours.

Thursday, December 22, 2005. John, Janice, and I were at the hospital in Harold's room today. The oncologist came in and told us that he was going to do a bone marrow test. He said it was needed because of the results of earlier tests. He let John help him as Janice and I watched. He was compassionate and insisted that we stay. The test took from one and one-half to two hours to perform.

When the results were in, the children talked to the oncologist privately. They told me the tests showed that the prostate cancer had invaded the neck of the bladder, and there was a large mass in the spleen.

The next day, Harold was still in the hospital in Atlanta. I came home for the evening. Shortly after I arrived home, the telephone rang. Reluctantly, I answered with a weak hello, and my world shattered. It was the oncologist.

"Your husband is dying of cancer," he said. His voice was deliberate and firm.

"No, it can't be!" my shaky voice replied.

The doctor's tone softened. "His only hope is to go on chemotherapy as soon as possible."

"Tomorrow is our wedding anniversary," I said between sobs. "Fifty-five years!"

He interrupted. "Then I have your permission to start the chemotherapy?"

"Oh, yes! When can you start?"

"Tomorrow."

My thoughts whirled as I began to realize what this meant for the future. I prayed for God's grace to cover me with strength, hope, and discernment. The possibility of not having Harold frightened me. Because of his past health issues, we had planned for this moment. But the reality of facing it *now* jarred me. My entire world would be torn apart.

Suddenly I was jolted back to reality. John was standing beside me. He tapped my shoulder and said, "Mom, are you okay?" He reassured me with a hug.

"I called all the family," he said. "We are having a chain prayer for Dad tonight at ten. I called Roger in

Memphis, and he is going to help me put this together. He remembered how our family prayed for him when he had cancer some years ago, and then the cancer went into remission."

The next day our lives changed. Janice, John, and I went together to the hospital to get instructions for bringing Harold home after the chemo treatment. By that time the other children were here, too: Debbie, Kevin, Cathy, and Diana. They gathered around our old oak table to make plans how to proceed in our present crisis.

Janice and Cathy developed an efficient way to manage. They put together Excel spreadsheets, called "Dad's Daily Health Log," "Dad's Daily Medication Log," "Dad's Daily Food," and "Daily Task List." These were all detailed reports to record vital statistics, medications, changes in symptoms, and food intake. They also made a list of telephone numbers of doctors, nurses, pharmacy, hospitals, and other helpers.

Next the children got out their Daily Task List. This list contained the instructions that they had gotten from the oncology nurse at the hospital for home care from Day 1 to Day 21 after each chemotherapy treatment. We were told that the chemotherapy would impair Harold's immune system severely, and any infection could lead to major complications. The instructions were detailed: Maintain good daily cleanliness. Keep Dad's bathroom sink and toilet disinfected with disposable wipes. Enter the bedroom only with a mask on face and latex gloves (after washing hands). Empty waste baskets. Wipe down door knobs and cabinet handles. Change bed linens and wash robe daily. Remove blankets and place in dryer on high for ten minutes to disinfect. On Day 14 Harold could leave the bedroom with a mask on. But all of the cleanliness rules should continue.

The entire crew immediately started the process. Kevin, Tim and John went shopping for the supplies we needed. The rest of us went through the house disinfecting everything. The master bedroom became Harold's hospital room. No one was allowed to come in until they put on a mask and latex gloves. Harold was confined to that room only. Cathy set him up with a stereo radio and CD system in addition to the TV and telephone. He was monitored day and night. Everyone took their turn.

The children stayed until they were satisfied that everything was in place for our lives to be as normal as possible. They planned to take turns to be here with us for Harold's chemotherapy treatments, scheduled for every twenty-one days for seven rounds.

By the middle of January, I started getting a painful rash. By the end of January, I went to the doctor, and she decided that I had shingles. This jolted me into the realization that I must take care of my own needs if I was going to help Harold during his greatest need. I decided to carve out more time at night to study God's Word and pray for discernment for each moment in my day.

In a few days, the youth minister at church, Rocky, brought the teenagers over to the house for a devotional. I prepared sandwiches, chips, and cookies. The event cheered Harold greatly. It uplifted our spirits and made me realize that God sends people to help us through our struggles. I thought of Psalm 139 and realized that God is here in our midst!

Tuesday, February 7, 2006. Harold has been depressed, so I found a three-ring binder and put his get-well cards in it in protective sheets. When I presented the binder to him, he smiled and was pleased. He especially liked the picture that I had taken of the teenagers when they had come for the devotional.

Throughout all of this a little voice inside me has kept saying, "Make everything as normal as possible."

When I don't know what else to do, I make schedules and spreadsheets of his changing medications and track his blood sugar, blood pressure, temperature, and any extraordinary side effects. Items that I do not schedule, Cathy and Janice do. That at least keeps us feeling that we are *doing* something!

By May, Harold had made a strong recovery, and he was anxious to get back to his normal activities. We decided to complete the household maintenance and organizational duties that we had been putting off.

We had new carpet installed all over the house. To get ready for the carpet layers, we were forced to clean out many things to give away or discard, and while they were working, the house was turned upside down.

When we had cleaned up the cluttered office, organized our file drawers, and sorted out the boxes of Harold's cassette tapes of sermons, we were finally ready to begin writing the book about our missionary journey to West Africa.

The end of May, our great-granddaughter had a birthday party in a town thirty minutes' drive away. She was two, and it was a special party outside in a park. It was a good party, but it completely exhausted Harold. Our hopes of Harold's continued recovery vanished quickly.

Suddenly we were back in the frenzy of new ailments and frequent visits to the doctor and the emergency room. Harold was an independent, persistent person, and he wasn't about to give up. Between symptoms, he climbed up on the roof and cleaned the gutter. He completed the greenhouse, repaired the plumbing under the kitchen sink, and replaced the azaleas at the side of the garage. He kept pressing on.

In the midst of all of this, his vision became increasingly worse. In the middle of June he made an appointment with his eye doctor, twelve miles away. He insisted that he could drive alone. So I went to the accounting office, and Harold went to his appointment. When I got home that night, Harold confronted me with another problem. As he was driving home on the freeway, a car in front of him stopped abruptly. Harold was unable to stop quickly enough, and he rear-ended the car. This was traumatic, because it signaled to him that his driving days were over. The diabetes, cancer, and mini-strokes had finally won out.

He continued his house maintenance projects and fell on the gravel at the back of our lot and skinned his arm and elbow badly. He said his feet got tangled up carrying lumber. Then while I was at the grocery store he washed all the windows in the sunroom.

We continued to be hopeful. Some of our children came at the end of June. It was an enormous boost to Harold's morale when he saw the faces of his beloved children: Janice, Tim and Cathy, and John.

July started out hopeful. While things seemed generally quiet, we felt this was the time to get our financial records in order, to review and revise our will, and to file our income tax before the extension came due. Harold was excited that John planned to come for his birthday on the twenty-third.

But things began to change around the middle of July. Harold's vision became worse, and he became unstable and began to run into things. He did not have any depth perception. He could see things, but he said they didn't seem to register in his brain. He said he couldn't focus or see well enough to read, lacked clarity of thought, and was plagued with headaches.

One night he fell in the bathroom and hit his head on the bathtub and made a large gash. We went to the emergency room, and they made stitches, bandaged his wounds, and took an MRI. They gave us the film and scheduled an appointment with a specialist for the next day. When I got him in the car the next day to see the specialist, I parked in the handicapped parking space, got his walker out, and tried to help him walk on the slightly uphill pavement. We both almost fell. A couple of men saw us and helped get him to the entrance, where a nurse helped him into a wheelchair.

He continued a downhill slide in his ability to be mobile. Later the doctor called and told me that he had studied the MRI and the news was bad—a large mass on the base of the skull. He prescribed new medication and advised us that Harold should see a neurologist. The mass could be cancer or a blood clot. If it was cancer, it would require radiation or even surgery.

Diana heard the news and came over to see her dad. We talked. Harold was so upbeat that we could not bear to tell him. We decided to let the doctor tell him. We continued to try to get the appointment to see a neurologist. His opinion would be more conclusive.

Harold became depressed and confused. He cried. Diana came over to see him. She seemed to help him. John called and encouraged him. Harold got up the next day feeling much better. We had a good day and talked most of the day.

In early August Harold's conversation seemed to turn to his duties when he had worked in civil service. He spoke extensively about his work in vibrations and molecular structure. Then he thanked me for listening

"That information and a quarter might get you a cup of coffee," he said. "Of all the things I miss, I miss my mind the most!"

He looked up and smiled and continued. "Thoughts have vibrations. Music has vibrations. Any sound has vibrations. We can control moods by music energy."

A few days later he said, "It's a good day. I got up and didn't see my name in the obituary."

Harold said that he can still see out of his left eye but not out of his right eye. He said he was very depressed and felt like crying. He complained of a headache. When we tried playing a game of canasta and he discovered that he couldn't do it, he cried. Janice and Luke both called, and Harold said he felt better.

One Sunday late in July we decided to stay home and have our service. I had prepared the communion bread and grape juice. We played a CD of one of his sermons and a music CD. I read scripture, and Harold prayed. We had communion and then discussed heaven and his sermons about the white stone in Revelation 2:17. At many of the churches where he had preached in the past, he had put a white quartz stone on the pulpit with the inscription, "Revelation 2:17." He would encourage people to keep on keeping on, and then they would receive the white stone. I got the white stone from his desk and we talked at length about it.

The next day we continued our Sunday discussion. We talked about *silence*. He said that silence is the absence of energy and there are no vibrations, no sound waves, no shock waves. There is nothing to stimulate and excite the external stimuli. God is working and he exercises these things, these vibrations. You can't hear sound waves but they are there. God is there but you can't see or hear him. Harold explained that he had tested metal and applied stress to see how much it could handle before it broke. He went on explaining in depth his work in vibration research.

Next morning he said he worked on it all night. He thanked me again and again for listening to him.

"Your hair is really growing," I said. "It's snow white, thick and wavy. I knew it would come back after your chemo treatments."

He chuckled. "Some bald-headed doctor will probably be envious and shave it off."

The next day we talked again.

"How many wives would bring their husband a glass of water the first thing every morning?" he said. "You are special!"

I smiled.

"I worked on solving the shower door problem last night," he said. "I've been using the shower door to pull myself up off the toilet and that's how it got out of adjustment."

Another night in his sleep he thought about how he had instrumented a propeller and how to get information off of the gauges.

He recalled vividly what he dreamed or what he thought in his sleep. We talked about resilient frequencies. He said he thought about it all night. Vibrations! Our voice stimulates brain activity. A

smile can affect things mentally. Eyes see it. This
stimulates the brain, and you feel better. Oh, the
energy a smile creates! The weather affects us—
sun—clouds—rain. The rays of the sun emit energy
that affects us. Our moods change drastically when
the sun comes up or goes down. It changes again
when the moon comes up. Everything that God has
set in order in our universe is amazing! What a
master mind! The lights in the house are pure
energy. Electrons are stimulated by electrical energy,
and it creates light. Science found what God made
and put it together. Magnificent minds were able to
put it together. I know so very, very little! The
inventors of the airplane saw birds fly. They studied
the structure and activity of the bird's wings. The all-
knowing mind yesterday set in order all things to
make today possible. I look at nature, the universe,
and all around me. That's my consolation! He knows!
This infinite source of energy knows all of this!

"Am I rambling like a lunatic again?" he asked. "If
I could step out of this body—what would it be like?"

He smiled and looked deeply into my eyes.

"I never thought about it before," I said.

A broad smile covered his face. "Whether in this
body or out of this body I really don't know—but I
heard unspeakable things. The energies. Words are
sounds. Words are thoughts, and not sounds—
energy. God spoke the world into existence. Process
to exercise energy. Do we understand that by using
words? Do we reduce that down to energy? Was it
words that made dry lands? Was it words that moved
the waters or the energy? Words become vehicles like

wires in electricity. Wires don't create electricity, energy does, but energy flows through the wires to make light."

Then he said, "I feel so comfortable sharing this with you."

Our eyes met, and I smiled.

"I wonder if all hurt energies are still inside or how pain is processed. The hurt caused by negative energies. Do they still linger? Is it part of the preservation process? A child burns a finger on a hot iron and remembers. Memories. Same thing. Don't want to get burned again. Words and energies."

Later that day we had our devotion. I played a dramatized version of Psalms 1–11. This seemed to refresh his spirit. I went downstairs to my office to research an upcoming doctor's visit. When I came upstairs again, Harold was sitting on the couch crying—sobbing. He told me that he had tried to fix the shower door and couldn't.

I breathed a silent prayer and gave him a hug. I went downstairs and grabbed a sermon tape and came back. It was a home Bible study that Harold had taught twenty years before. The subject was patience. So God spoke words of comfort to Harold that day from Harold's own voice.

Sunday, August 6, 2006. Harold was very depressed today. When I came into the sunroom, he was sitting on the couch with his head bowed, crying.

I sat beside him, put my arm around his shoulder, and held him tight. When his sobbing stopped, I asked if he would still like to have the Sunday devotion we had planned. He nodded yes.

I read Psalm 1, and we sang a verse of "I Shall Not Be Moved" and "The Lord Is My Shepherd." Then I read John 14:1–2 (TLB):

> Let not your heart be troubled. You are trusting God, now trust in Me. There are many homes up there where my Father lives, and I am going to prepare them for your coming. When everything is ready, then I will come and get you, so that you can always be with Me where I am. If this weren't so, I would tell you plainly. And you know where I am going and how to get there.

Harold worded a prayer as we held hands. I served communion. Then we sat awhile talking about how God had blessed us. Afterward he cried again and told me about his doubts and struggles and how his mind was playing tricks on him. Then we cried together and held hands.

Wednesday, August 9, 2006. Ray came over this morning at ten to take Harold, Diana, and me to Harold's neurologist appointment. After the consultation the neurologist was concerned about doing the brain biopsy because the medicine that he gives after surgery to reduce the swelling around the brain would drastically raise Harold's already high blood-sugar levels. He recommended that we consult the oncologist before we started any treatment. We should weigh risks against benefits.

Debbie has arranged for a large family-wide chain prayer tonight at ten.

Friday, August 10, 2006. Last night Harold fell while going to the bathroom. I woke at three and heard him. I bandaged his wounds. We talked a few minutes, and then he drifted off in sleep.

Today I sat in the recliner in the sunroom, and Harold lay on the couch with his head propped up on a pillow.

He started talking again. "God is an inexhaustible source of energy like the sunshine . . . Jesus . . . he promised energy to his disciples to do things. Energy is from God. The disciples were instruments to transfer energy to others—like the sun. I enjoyed the sun yesterday. It was like God was saying, 'I am here!' Job asked why, but he didn't blame God. God doesn't enjoy our suffering—but Satan does. Heaven . . . Satan cannot go there. He cannot go back. Hope! Beauty! Some things God cannot change, but he gives us energy to get through it. Principles and laws set up by God, and God the Infinite Source has power to do it, but because of Infinite Wisdom cannot do it. Beautiful principles. Infinite Source of Energy! God's Energy! My hope is that everything has a reason and a purpose and that the Infinite Source of Energy will accomplish his purpose in me. It is staggering to know that we are God's children and because of that we have access to his infinite source of energy by faith. Faith to move mountains!"

Then he said, "We are gods but die as men."

Saturday, August 12, 2006. This morning I sat in the recliner in the sunroom and looked at Harold lying on the couch with his head propped on the pillow.

He looked up at me and said, "I like to be seen with you and to look at the envy in the face of other men."

I saw the twinkle in his brown eyes as I viewed his face over the rim of my coffee cup. I tried to smile and his face blurred through my teary eyes. Oh, how I am going to miss him! I set my cup down and I prayed to be strong for him. He was always strong for me.

"That Infinite Wisdom that we call God," he said. "We are so blessed! I wanted the children to go to Africa. They needed that experience. Now we have a great relationship. That experience bonded us into a great team."

He got a faraway look in his eyes and stopped talking for a moment.

"Luck infuriates me!" he said with an angry voice. "Someone called and said, 'Good luck on your surgery.' Saying good luck means that we do not believe in a Supreme Being that lives in us and works in our lives. How can people say they believe and act the opposite? Elohim—everything made by God. Sometimes I struggle with Romans 8:28. I think why this? Then I go back to the starting point. There has to be a Supreme Energy—a Being that put all things together. How can we challenge him? That's where confidence and knowledge is. He knows what he is doing. Job is the oldest book in the Bible. Men have been asking that question for a long time. We've heard, 'Never question God.' But God gave us that ability, and he expects us to ask why. In church—don't ask questions! Flawed thinking! Nuclear fusion. God put it there and man discovered it. God directed him to understand it. God wants us to think. He is like a father that wants his son to imitate him."

This evening when Harold and I talked, he said, "Yesterday when I figured out about the flapper in the tank in the toilet, it worked. That's important! I figured out how to do it, and I did it. It was very encouraging to me. I know what to do. I know how to do it, and I looked to find just the right rubber band to do it. So encouraging. Just a rubber band."

I took his temperature, his blood pressure, and his sugar level. Then he started talking again.

"When I go out with you in the car, I get so frustrated." He chuckled. "No, it's not your driving."

His expression changed quickly and I could hear the anxiety in the tone of his voice.

"I recognize the names of the roads, but I don't know where they are. I must learn all over again. I get so frustrated. Know names—can't remember where they are. That's why the rubber band experience was so important. The rubber band brings such peace of mind."

His eyes got that faraway look and he continued.

"Right at our fingertips is the knowledge of the Supreme Being and he knows it. Let this mind be in you that was in Christ Jesus. Where did Einstein's mind come from, or Bill Gates's? It came from the infinite Supreme Being. Because at this time, God wanted that information out. Gasoline. Oil. God created it and put it in the earth and guided man to

find it and find a use for it. That's why he created
them. Man can't make oil. Not really. I thank God for
Model T Fords running down the road. How much
more is out there that we don't know about? What
else has that Energy and Mind created?"

Before bed I bandaged his face and arm from his
fall last night and changed the dressing. Then we
slowly made our way to the bedroom. He gripped his
cane in one hand and tightly held my arm with his
other hand.

Sunday, August 13, 2006. When Harold got up
this morning, he was very talkative. He started out
by saying, "Our spirit returns to God who gave it. We
existed before we were born. Our spirit is from God
and is eternal. He knew us before we were born and
knew what we would do. He gave us talents and
characteristics to do what he wants us to do. Isn't
God wonderful? I prayed that God would show us the
purpose for our life and lead us in that direction."

I kept thinking, "His spiritual thoughts are *very*
clear even though he asks me to show him what to
do every day and what to eat and what to wear."

He has increasing difficulty moving around. He
uses a cane or a walker. I help him get dressed. He
seems to rely on me for everything. He keeps telling
me, "You are an angel. You are a gift from God to me.
You are beautiful!" He says this to me every day.
"What would I do without you?" he says. What an
awesome responsibility I have!

We tried to go to church. I helped him shave.

He said, "Shaving is a manly thing and then I feel so good."

After breakfast I helped him get dressed. He decided to rest on the couch. I attempted to get ready to go. Later when I peeked in to check on him, he was asleep. The song "There is a Balm in Gilead" softly floated through the entire room through the surround-sound stereo system.

Tuesday, August 15, 2006. Harold had a headache again this morning behind his eyes. His mouth is sore. He feels cold at night and wants a blanket. When he wakes up, I get him a robe to keep him warm. He didn't sleep last night. He didn't take a sleeping pill. He said my snoring kept him awake.

He woke up at six, and I helped him to the couch in the sunroom.

He said, "It's so comfortable here. I love you, Mother. I love you so very, very much. We count our blessings now!"

By seven he was asleep on the couch.

I went to my office downstairs to begin again the horrible ordeal of trying to confirm the appointment with the oncologist and the conference call from the girls.

Harold keeps saying, "Life is a memory."

Saturday, August 19, 2006. Harold fell yesterday in the bathroom. He was putting a wash cloth on the towel rack. He asked me to go downstairs to the patio and fix the water fountain. The water had quit flowing. He said to hit the pipe with a hammer until the water started again. Then I heard a loud noise. Harold had fallen. He couldn't get up. I tried to get him up, but he was too heavy. I called Diana, and she came over, and we were both able to get him up. Willie, our neighbor, came over. He said that he felt something was wrong and wanted to offer his help. Harold was always happy to see Willie. After their visit, Willie told us that he was only a phone call away if we needed more help. After Willie left, Diana came over again. We helped Harold get to the table. We had a very enjoyable meal together. Later, after Diana left, I helped him take his shower— got him to bed and set up with a urinal. He *promised* to ring the bell so I could help him use it by the bed. I went downstairs to work, and sure enough—the pitter-patter of feet. He was up again in the bathroom.

Monday, August 21, 2006. On our journey, God has sent his servants to help us cope with the various stages of cancer, and we give praises to such a gracious and merciful God.

Our journey has now led to a fork in the road: after several months of lymphoma remission, the cancer is back as a large growth in Harold's brain. It affects his motor skills. Loss of balance. Limited use of left side of his body. Difficulty walking. Headaches. He is like a stroke victim.

We have consulted several doctors about options: internist, neurosurgeon, oncologist, cardiologist. As usual, we have had a family conference. This time our children moved into the leadership role. Cathy and Janice arranged for a conference call with the neurosurgeon and then did internet research. Shauna asked the doctor, and he rearranged his schedule to get Harold in quickly. Armed with the girl's information, I strongly urged the oncologist to see us as soon as possible. He was booked up through October. Prayers of many saints caused him to cancel some appointments and make room for us near the end of the day two days later. He also agreed to talk to Cathy and Janice with a conference call while we were in the doctor's office. Diana drove us to the appointment in Marietta and heard the conference also. The doctor patiently addressed all the issues and the concerns the girls had for an hour and a half.

After the conference phone call ended, the oncologist explained to Harold the options that were available. He did not believe that a biopsy of the brain would add enough information to merit the risk of the surgery. He said that he highly recommended a new experimental type of chemotherapy. He said that the risks were quite high for this clinical trial but he said that he believed that Harold should try all means available to stay alive as many days or weeks as possible. He said that this aggressive cancer needed treatment immediately.

Without blinking an eye, Harold quickly responded, "I do not want to continue this treatment. I am a Christian. I have tried to serve Christ faithfully all of my life. I know where I am going. I am not afraid."

The oncologist stared silently for a few moments, then walked out of the room without looking back.

Chapter 3
Black Storm Clouds

For You will light my lamp; The Lord my God will enlighten my darkness.
—Psalm 18:28 (NKJV)

Thursday, August 24, 2006. I arranged today to set Harold up with hospice care. Harold's only request was that he remain at home with me. He said that he was ready to go see his Heavenly Father and Jesus Christ in Heaven. Our thoughts have been moved from hope to heaven. This has been a confirmation of what we had already known in our hearts. This caused us to get into action mode. Cathy is coming tomorrow to help.

I called our doctor at eight this morning and by 8:30 she had arranged for hospice to come. Hospice workers came at 10:30 and the nurse stayed until 5:30 this evening. Now I am in the local hospital emergency room waiting while they install a catheter for Harold. The nurse tried at home but could not do it. The emergency room nurse is trying now.

Willie and Marie came this morning. Willie had come at six to help Harold go to the bathroom, and then Willie and Marie came back together. Janice and Cathy called. Diana brought Katherine and Nathan over. Helen and Stuart came and brought food. They stayed yesterday all day. Charles and Jo

Ann came and helped set up the hospice furniture—hospital bed, oxygen, other equipment. Yesterday Kurt came and set up an intercom. Jack brought over a wheel chair.

Harold left for the hospital in an ambulance around five. I got to the emergency room at 5:30. It is six now and he is still being helped.

Several people called today. I have had phone calls constantly. It is difficult to get things done. Harold calls me constantly for urgent problems. He is so sweet—still joking—his mind is sharp, but his motor skills are deteriorating.

Late night. I waited impatiently while they kept trying to install the catheter. We went in at 5:30 and did not get out until 11:30. After several extremely painful attempts, they called the urologist. He decided to insert the catheter surgically in his abdomen. More intense pain. The ambulance brought us home.

The minute Harold was admitted to hospice care, everything changed. Hospice workers came to the house, assessed our needs, and made recommendations. We moved the special bed and equipment into the sunroom and converted it into Harold's hospital room. This allowed him to view the entire back of the house, be in the sunshine, and watch the squirrels, rabbits, and stray dogs play outside—maybe even a young deer or two. He could also see the arbor he had built and where he had married a daughter and grandchildren.

The room also made it easy for him to visit with the people he loved. He had specifically built the room for this purpose ten or more years before. He filled the room with beautiful plants and built a small fountain below so he could watch the birds come for a drink. His American Indian heritage gave him a deep love for nature.

The hospice workers were a deep comfort to us. We knew that Harold was getting good care and that he was able to be home with family and friends. I suddenly felt the urgency to make each moment count or it would be lost forever. Hospice workers are taking care of all of Harold's physical needs. The children are enjoying those last special moments with their beloved Daddy. When the life that Harold and I had shared together flashed before my eyes, I could see all the many people that he had loved from many surrounding churches where he had served. I knew that they would want to tell him goodbye and I know that he would savor each moment of their loving attention. So I slipped away from everyone and spent hours in my downstairs office inviting people to come and tell Harold goodbye.

As soon as the church learned that Harold was in hospice, they provided food every day. Visitors came every day, to Harold's delight. After I saw Harold's countenance as he talked to the visitors, I was so glad that I had made those phone calls. I heard him say, "I'm dying, and I love every minute of it."

After I saw this, I slipped away alone and made the funeral arrangements. Since we were in the beginning of the hospice process, I felt that I would be better able to deal with the last days if I got the emotional ordeal of arranging the funeral over in a rational manner. Kurt highly recommended Byers Funeral Home, and Jim from work recommended Sawnee View Memorial Gardens. Marty Byers could not have been kinder. He sat with me in his office, cried with me and prayed. Later he came to the house to see if he could help with any other arrangements.

Our children met again around the oak table and made plans. They thought that my mind was operating in a fog. They decided first of all that I could not handle the situation without help. So our daughter Janice took a family leave from work and stayed with me.

The children got a new cell phone for me with all of their numbers programmed into the phone. They arranged for lawn care, installed a new security system, had our vehicles serviced, and reviewed the house maintenance information that Harold had provided for me.

By Saturday, September 2, family started arriving from their homes from coast to coast. We had sixteen for supper: Denise, Rosemary, Amanda, Joseph, Katherine, Diana, Nathan, Natalia, Jeremy, Shauna, John, Jim, Harold, and I. John and Tim prepared barbecue ribs, and Janice potato salad. Katherine made slaw and a lemon cake. I made a tossed salad. We held hands around Harold's bed, and he said a prayer. He had a faraway look. He calls everyone beautiful. Many others came in later: Tara, Shane and Bailey, Cathy, Rachelle and Helene, Debbie and Kevin.

Sunday morning we decided to have a family devotion around Harold's bed. John read the fourteenth chapter of the Gospel of John. Tim served communion after Harold said a few words and prayed. Afterward, Harold presented a short lesson on love. John said a closing prayer. All of a sudden, Harold burst out singing, "What the world needs now is love, sweet love. It's the only thing that there's just too little of. What the world needs now is love, sweet love . . ."

Visitors came from church that afternoon. Later Amanda and Joseph stood at Harold's bedside tearfully telling him good-bye before they left for their home in Las Cruces, New Mexico. At the same time, Nathan, our three-year-old great grandson was at the other side of the room playing with a new toy that made loud, crazy noises.

Later that night we called the nurse because Harold had started having seizures. The nurse said to lay him on his side and place something in his mouth until the seizure passed.

Monday was Labor Day. We ate a late brunch, and all the company left to go home except Janice and Tim. Harold slept most of the day. Janice and Tim gave him a sponge bath, shampooed his hair, and changed his bed. Janice decided to stay on and help take care of her Daddy. Tim flew to his business trip to Boston.

It was a great comfort to have Janice with us. She quite capably managed everything. She helped the hospice workers, greeted visitors, and answered the telephone. She insisted on sleeping on the couch near Harold's bed so I would get a good night's sleep.

Saturday, September 9, 2006. Yesterday Debbie and Kevin came. Kevin insisted on inspecting Harold's truck and my car and working on house repairs. Debbie comforted her Dad by massaging his cramping calves and his forehead and temples, attempting to ease his terrible headache.

Harold is slipping fast. This morning he slept a lot. By early afternoon we couldn't get him to wake up— even while changing his bed. We called hospice. The nurse came by at seven. She was from Nigeria. We got Harold to stir a little. The nurse said to stop all medicine except two. This was a great milestone for us to stop giving him all of the numerous medications, vitamins, and blood sugar medication, and only give him medication to keep him as comfortable and free from pain as possible. She said he could have all the sugar he wanted. The nurse assured us that they never left enough pain medication that would cause his death, but only enough to make him comfortable. The message pierced our hearts, as we began to comprehend the words. We were stunned as we faced the inevitable outcome—he only has a very short time with us.

Sunday, September 10, 2006. We had our devotional around Harold's bed. Kevin read John 14. We had communion and a short prayer. Harold was still very sleepy. Visitors came in the afternoon, and some brought food.

The children are giving thought to funeral plans. They have asked me to pick out the songs. One that I have chosen is "The Joy of the Lord Is Our Strength."

Thursday, September 14, 2006. Harold has stopped eating. He still sleeps a lot. When the hospice nurse came, Janice asked how long she thought Harold would live. The nurse said she was surprised he was still alive. She said that she thought he was waiting for us to tell him good-bye. We looked puzzled. The nurse told us to think about it.

Friday, September 15, 2006. Janice woke us all at three this morning, saying that she had been awake for two hours talking to Harold. He kept telling her about the beautiful sights he was seeing. He kept reaching his arms out as if he was trying to touch someone. He wanted the air bed mattress turned off because the noise disturbed him. He asked her to turn off the oxygen. He said, "Turn off my breath." She said that Harold wanted to talk to us. Janice, Cathy, John, and I all gathered around his bed. We were stunned to see him sitting up with his arms outstretched to the sky after being in a coma. For several hours Janice and Cathy cheered him on saying, "Take hold of Jesus' hand It's your time! Reach up and take hold of Jesus' hand and he will take you there." John joined in the cheering section. I promised him that I would complete the book telling of our missionary experiences in West Africa. We all gave him a hug and a kiss and gave him permission to leave. He said a few words. Then the expression on his face totally changed. He looked peaceful and happy.

Speaking clearly and in a passionate tone of voice, he said, "God's house! Beautiful! Let's Go!"

I was stunned with cold chills as I witnessed the expression on his face.

Janice said, "He is so ready but something is holding him here."

Cathy said, "Tonight is not a good night to die. This is just a dress rehearsal."

Cathy and I went back to bed. John insisted on sleeping in the recliner near his Dad's bed. He told Janice, "I do not want you to be alone."

Saturday, September 16, 2006. Barbara, his nurse, came early. She said again that Harold was waiting for someone. She asked if all of the children were here. Janice told her that Debbie was not here. Later Janice called Debbie in North Carolina. "Debbie, I know that you cannot be here. I am going to hold the phone up to Dad's ear. He can't talk but he will be able to hear you. Tell him that you love him." Debbie said, "Dad, I love you and know we will see each other again. It's okay. You are only going first." After this conversation, Harold has seemed to be in a deep coma. Many people have come by to visit, bring food, and pray as we have continued our vigil. John cut the grass this morning. This afternoon he insisted that all of us gather around Harold's bed, hold hands, and pray. John led the prayer. It was sweet. He broke down several times and cried—then silence—but he got through the prayer.

Later this afternoon I took Harold's clothing to the funeral home, along with his military papers, an obituary the children had written, and a picture.

Monday, September 18, 2006. Janice's birthday! Harold slept the night with oxygen—with labored breathing. We gave him his pain medication at 10:30 and I took a quick shower. I checked on him at eleven. His blood pressure was 40 over 33, and his pulse was 40. A few minutes later the door bell rang. Kurt had come to see him. When we got to Harold's bedside, we discovered together that Harold had stopped breathing. I did not find him alone; Kurt was there. Kurt prayed.

In a moment the phone rang. It was Harold's special nurse, Shalandra, calling on her day off. When she heard what had just happened, she came and cleaned him up, gave him a shave, and shampooed his hair. Her day off. I called Marty Byers to come. Barbara, his nurse called. When I told her that Harold had died and the funeral director was coming to take him away she said, "You can't take him away until I sign off on his death!"

Barbara immediately came, signed the proper documents and gathered up the pain medication and flushed them down the toilet. She called to have the equipment removed immediately.

Shortly after Barbara's car pulled out of the driveway, I saw the black funeral hearse slowly inch its way toward the front porch.

Janice was sitting in the swing with Cathy. "Go inside, Mom," Janice said, "and open up the sunroom door. I'll tell them to go to the back door."

I opened the sunroom door and looked tenderly at the stiff, cold body in the bed. I walked over to touch him and stooped down to kiss his forehead one more time. I was interrupted abruptly by the two men who were rolling the gurney through the back door just as Marty Byers walked with Janice into the room. Cathy trailed behind.

I tried to say something but I stood silently in disbelief. In a few moments it was over.

After they left, I could feel that his presence—that energy of his—was gone. I wondered if this was a dream or a nightmare. It was like viewing the devastation after an earthquake or hurricane.

Before I could collect my thoughts, the doorbell rang. The hospice workers had come to remove the hospital bed, the oxygen equipment, the bedside table, and the wheel chair. Afterwards Janice, Tim, Cathy, John, Debbie, and Kevin arranged the room to accommodate visitors as they dropped by. Everything suddenly began moving very fast as the children and I started to finalize the memorial service, welcome the out-of-town guests, plan meals, and plan the children's next visit during Thanksgiving Week.

When I was finally alone and had time to catch my breath, I wondered how I would get through the ordeal of the viewing and the funeral. I prayed!

Chapter 4
After the Storm

Your word is a lamp for my feet, a light on my
path.

—Psalm 119:105

The day of the funeral was a bright sunshiny fall
day. As we walked across the church parking lot
toward the building, I looked up at the beautiful deep
blue sky and then noticed the newly planted flowers
in front of the building. I was surprised to see so
many cars in the parking lot and wondered why.

Although we had arrived early, when we entered
the church building we heard music. Bruce
Warmbrod was making final preparations for a media
display. He had worked patiently for hours with the
children to make a musical pictorial of Harold's life
for display in the foyer and on the projection screen
in the front of the sanctuary. The songs he had
picked to accompany the presentation were "God Will
Make a Way," "Let Me Be a Sacrifice," "Gentle
Shepherd," "On Bended Knee I Come," "Amazing
Grace," and "Bring Him Home."

While the children met with Bruce, I browsed
down the hall and saw women in the kitchen
preparing a meal for our family to eat before the
funeral service. My heart was overwhelmed with

gratitude for the acts of kindness shown to us during Harold's sickness and death.

Later, after our family ate the delicious meal prepared for us, we were led to a room to wait for the usher to take us to the sanctuary to be seated. My mind was a blur as my body went through the motions of waiting. After what seemed an eternity, we were all ushered into the sanctuary. We walked past Harold's casket. A bright blue, gold, fuchsia, and green kente cloth was draped over the end. I touched the kente gently and looked at Harold's lifeless body. My sobbing and tears were uncontrollable. I caught my breath, prayed a silent prayer, and felt God releasing a new spirit in me. I sat down beside Janice.

Rocky Wyatt, the song leader, stood and welcomed everyone and thanked them on behalf of the family for coming. He said that Harold was a man of God and always had a personal walk with God. Then he led us in singing "My God and I" and "The Joy of the Lord Is Our Strength."

When I saw Shane Miller walking toward the pulpit, I felt another wave of tears coming on. Shane was the preacher who had succeeded Harold at the Etowah River Church of Christ. I started focusing on the words of the song, "The Joy of the Lord Is Our Strength," and kept repeating the words over and over again in my thoughts with every fiber in my body. In a few minutes, I was able to regain my composure.

After the song, Shane said that he felt he was family. He read the obituary, and then he said:

"I stand before you as Harold's Timothy. It was such a joy for me to know Harold. Harold will always be the minister of Etowah River Church. Everything he did—the buildings, the land, his philosophy— everything had his signature all over it, and Miss Jane's. All of the country is thankful to them for the year after year, year after year, they served in ministry to Jesus Christ.

"When I started preparing this I tried to make notes. Then I thought, if I need notes, then I didn't learn anything. I have memories and all that Harold meant to me. He was a minister to everyone. I talked to Janie Brumbelow in the audience. She is ninety and still talks about all that Harold meant to her. My daughter is nine and still talks about some of the lessons that Harold taught.

"People were not only attracted to his personality, but to him as a man of God. He was like Moses. He sacrificed much to spread the kingdom of God.

"What I remember most is the time I first met Harold. The church met in a little white building, and no one could go out that door without getting a hug from Harold—a six-foot-five three-hundred-pounder or a five-foot-two. Harold made everyone feel special. Harold changed our lives. We met in his sunroom for Bible studies. Many of these studies focused on the teachings in the parables. Harold always had a different, distinctive message, thanks be to God, because of the many years he had prayerfully studied the Bible. He had spent fifty-four years in the Word. He often spoke about death—the subject we have the most difficulty discussing. He would always say that we fall asleep in Jesus. He would point to his body and say, 'This is not Harold Derr. This is just the envelope that I am temporarily using. The real Harold Derr is inside.' He would often read 1 Corinthians 6:19 and Romans 6:6–10. Harold lives in each and every one of our memories.

"During one of our business meetings, Harold said that he needed to be out of town the next Sunday. He said he needed someone to preach, and he looked straight at me. He kept gazing at me, and I reluctantly did it. I did it because I loved Harold so much.

"The message that he taught most frequently was the parable of the ten virgins as taught in Matthew 25:1–13. Harold's messages were always different and insightful. Harold said that the oil in the parable represented the influence we have on each other. Harold's influence goes much further than the people who are here, friends and family. It goes to a much larger group, from Ghana, West Africa, to all of the other places that Harold preached. His lamp will always burn brightly in each of us until the Lord comes."

Then Shane prayed, and Rocky led us in two more songs, "Faithful Love" and "When We All Get to Heaven." During the songs I could feel Janice becoming anxious. I wondered why. Before the service, the children had huddled together in the foyer. Then the service began, and there had been no opportunity for us to talk.

Kurt Picker, the senior minister at Grace Chapel Church of Christ, went to the pulpit next.

"What a blessing to be able to celebrate a faithful servant of the Lord," Kurt said. "I have never before had the opportunity to preach the funeral for a preacher of the gospel—a preacher who faithfully preached until he died. I feel his presence.

"Preachers have come and worshipped where I was before, and they were not very supportive. I guess they thought that they could do it better. And I was intimidated by the years that Harold had faithfully preached. I never asked why he didn't stay at Etowah River. I wondered if there was a problem. But when I heard Shane today, I understood. Harold knew that if he had stayed at Etowah, he would have still been the preacher, and he knew that the congregation needed to start relying on Shane.

"Harold was a very humble man and a man of great character. I saw that in his illness. He was a man of great faith. Psalm 116:15 says, 'Precious in the sight of the Lord is the death of his saints.'

"I thought about this message and wondered what Harold would want me to say. I think that he would want me to just present the simple gospel that he had preached for so many years."

Then Kurt read Romans 8:1–4 and verse 11: "Therefore, there is now no condemnation for those who are in Christ Jesus, because through Christ Jesus the law of the Spirit of life set me free from the law of sin and death. For what the law was powerless to do in that it was weakened by the sinful nature, God did by sending his own Son in the likeness of sinful man to be a sin offering. And so he condemned sin in sinful man, in order that the righteous requirements of the law might be fully met in us, who do not live according to the sinful nature but according to the Spirit . . . And if the Spirit of him who raised Jesus from the dead is living in you he who raised Christ from the dead will also give life to your mortal bodies through his Spirit who lives in you."

Then Kurt said, "Harold spoke often and comfortably about the love of God. That was the message that he preached over and over again. His children would like to come now and present their memories of their father and their daddy."

I sat stunned as the girls slowly walked up to the pulpit—Janice, Diana, Cathy, and Debbie. I had known that Janice was to share some stories and pictures, but I wondered why the other girls were with her. They had not told me about this.

Debbie stepped forward and spoke first.

"My father was a visionary," she said, "a big-picture thinker, and a dreamer. He was passionate about fulfilling all of those dreams. His passion for God started even before he met my mother. He was baptized just after their wedding rehearsal in the Church of Christ in Terre Haute, Indiana. The first sermon he preached was in Biloxi, Mississippi, just a few weeks later. The sermon was from Revelation and was about the second coming of Jesus Christ.

"As children we realized how paramount God was in his life. Before school at the breakfast table we read a chapter from *Hurlbut's Story of the Bible*. We had devotionals several times a week. Dad frequently cited parables that told that we reap what we sow, and he particularly emphasized what happened when we made the wrong choices."

Then Janice spoke.

"Dad was a very generous man. He shared his time and his resources even when those resources were scarce. He was such a giver. I remember him giving away some of our own possessions. He gave away furniture. He invited a young woman in Terre Haute, Indiana, to come live with us—for two years, in fact. She came from a needy family that could not help her to fulfill her dream of going to college. Dad saw her potential and wanted to help her attain that worthy goal. So she came to live with us. She was able to graduate from college.

"As children we had to share our father, and sometimes that was tough. He was all about making sacrifices and about sharing the Word. That was very dear to him. We had some wonderful marvelous experiences. A wonderful memory to me was spending time at the lake house. Dad's parents owned a cabin on a large lake nearby. We had some wonderful memories there. Our cousin Denise is sitting in the audience. She remembers. One vivid memory was of our fishing experience. Dad loved to fish and to spend time with his parents and family. But not everyone in the family enjoyed fishing. Dad had a way of getting us all on board. He was a very enthusiastic, charismatic man. He even worked on his children sometimes. Many week-ends we would go to the lake house, and he would have us all get in the boat. He had convinced us we were going to have the time of our life. We didn't. We really didn't. Diana hated to fish. John was the only one who liked it, and he was the only one who caught anything. Dad spent the entire time putting worms on hooks and untangling lines. But I bet he had the time of his life anyway."

I laughed at this memory and began to swell with pride. It was becoming obvious that each of the girls would speak, and that they had devoted time, love, and prayers to their presentation. I was told later that they had stayed up nearly the whole night before, getting ready. They had rushed me off to bed early, "to rest." I had thought they just wanted to visit, but no, they had been preparing these stories, and I sat amazed at what each one told.

Janice was still speaking. "One of our adventures," she said, "involved winter in Indiana. Dad built an oversized sled and tied it behind our car. We all got onboard and he drove us through the streets of our neighborhood. We thought that was a blast. Then he told us that we were going to take the sled to the lake house, and we were going to ride the sled down the hill and onto the icy lake below. We thought this was a grand plan. When we tried it, I thought we were going to kill ourselves. In fact, I think Mom took the sled away from Dad after that. Yes, we had a very bad accident! But I remember that as one of our wonderful adventures with Dad.

"We went on several vacations together, many of them between preaching assignments. Dad wanted to spread much knowledge and wanted to start churches, and then when they got on their feet he wanted to move on. So our family had many marvelous opportunities to see wonderful sights like the Grand Canyon.

"We had the marvelous opportunity as a family to be missionaries in Ghana, West Africa. The seed for this was planted by a Sunday school teacher that my father had. He always had in his heart the desire to preach the Word. At one point in time, we were going to go to New Zealand. That didn't work out, so Dad wanted to go somewhere else. The mission was in Ghana, West Africa, in the 60s, and he really wanted to model our family after the Apostle Paul. So he convinced the church that this was a good plan for our family. However, a part of the challenge was that we had to provide money for our travel fund. We had to go to churches just like this one to try to raise funds. We pulled our seventeen-foot travel trailer behind our International Harvester, and we went from San Diego, California, to Wilmington, Delaware, raising funds. It was an adventure for sure.

"One story that stands out in my mind is this one. Frequently we would park our trailer in church parking lots or trailer parks. This time we were in Barstow, California. Dad had just preached a compelling message about sharing the good news of the gospel to Ghana. Then as usual, our family got up and sang 'I Know the Lord Will Find a Way for Me.' Sometimes we would also sing 'Kum Bah Yah.' Very compelling. Sometimes there was not a dry eye in the place. So we had just made the presentation. We went to our travel trailer, and Mom held up a can of peaches and said, 'Kids, here's a can of peaches.

We have six dollars to our name. This is for food and gasoline.'

"Dad said, 'We'd better start praying!' So our family had a prayer session. Dad just knew that God was going to come through, but we had doubts. In just a short time, three young couples knocked on our door and wondered how we were doing. Dad very elegantly told our immediate needs. These couples then gave us forty-six dollars, enough to get us to our next destination. So we were on our way. That's how my dad lived his life. Give him a goal, and you had better stand back because he was going to achieve it. To him the journey was as important as the destination—the journey through life. That was really a lot of fun. We actually made it to Ghana, West Africa.

"We were in Ghana about two years, during politically challenging times. My dad had a vision to teach in a preacher training school. There was nowhere that Dad said we couldn't go in our VW van. Sometimes we all got out and pushed the VW. Not only did we go back into primitive villages, but we loved to sightsee. Dad was quite an adventurer. The kente on the casket is a prize possession. It was woven by hand in Ghana. A cloth like this is only given to people of stature.

"We had to get used to snakes, smelly stench, spiders, and lizards. Sometimes in the remote villages people had never seen white children, so they would like to touch us. Dad loved diversity. He had concerns for peoples' physical healing and dispensed malaria medicine, bandages, and vitamins. Mom gave out chewing gum.

"Dad decided to have a vacation Bible school. We didn't think it would fly, because it was too much of a European concept. But Dad convinced us it would work. He got us all on board, and we sat at a little desk in the garage office and cut out literally hundreds of crowns. When we gave out the crowns at VBS, everyone wanted a crown of glory. Many people attended the VBS every day, even the chiefs of the village, and everyone—even the chief—wanted a crown. They were so open to the gospel and open to the Word and the entire village wanted a crown. When we visited this village months later, the people were still wearing the crowns. Talk about planting seeds that go on forever! That was amazing to me."

Then Cathy went to the pulpit and spoke.

"Dad always made mention of how receptive the Ghanaians were to the Word of God, and he would sometimes talk about how disappointed he was when he came back to the States and found that people here were not as receptive. It excited him to talk about how receptive the people were in Ghana. That was very precious to him.

"As Debbie said earlier, Dad was all about God. There was also a human side to him. My parents had children very early in life—five children. It was the 60s, and we had come back from Ghana to live in the Mojave Desert. Dad had the magical quality of making everything positive. He was always a half-full kind of guy. We came back from Ghana and we had nothing. No clothes. No shoes. But we did have a house provided by the church. The members brought us sofas, lamps, and beds. A truck pulled up in front of the house with clothes. Diana got up into the truck, looked over the sizes, and tossed clothes down to us as we scampered to find our right size. Dad had convinced us children that we were really very wealthy. It was a convincing story, because we had just come back from Ghana where the people were naked and starving. It was a stark contrast for us.

"Another great thing about Dad was that ministers don't have a nine-to-five work week. Dad made us breakfast, had a devotional, and he was there for us when we came home from school. At least as a minister he had the flexibility to do that.

"You don't make very much on a minister's salary. So my mother started working soon after we came back to the States. This is the message that all of us children took home. Mother would say 'There's so much to be thankful for.' "

Cathy wiped the tears from her eyes and went on. "All of us were grateful. It didn't matter how much we had, we were always grateful. That's what I tell my own children today. In Ghana we always had tremendous health. We took numerous vaccinations, but we didn't have any serious injuries. We had over six hundred kinds of poisonous snakes, but we never got a snake bite. That's what I keep drilling into my children," Cathy said through tears. "There's so much to be grateful for."

Janice returned to the pulpit and continued.

"The human side of Dad was when we came back to the States. Soon we moved to a suburb of Los

Angeles. It was a time of long hair, beards, and the hippy movement. There were a lot of external dynamics going on. The three older Derr girls were teenagers now and had started dating. My parents tried so hard to be great parents. Dad tried so hard to teach his children the right way and to teach with dynamics. Dad always emphasized the immutable laws of God and that he was not going to turn back the clock for us—The Law of Consequences. 'I will give you guidelines,' he said, 'and I expect you to follow them. I won't cancel out your consequences.'

"Diana was my partner in crime. We traveled so frequently that our sisters were our best friends. Once we decided that we wanted to go out, as we did often in the evening. We stayed out past our curfew of ten o'clock. We were pulled over by the police! I don't know who was crying harder, Diana or me. Of course tears and women and police officers usually work, but God had another plan for us that Dad was a part of. We were arrested, and the policeman put us in his squad car and took us to the local jail. In the waiting room we were crying and begging them, 'Call our parents. Call our parents.'

"The police officer opened up a filthy jail cell and put us in and slammed the door shut. We looked at each other and said, 'It was only curfew. We didn't do drugs. We didn't drink alcohol. It was only curfew!' We waited and we cried. We waited and we cried. We saw the little toilet in the corner and said, 'We are not going to do that. We will hold it.' The other officers would come by and peer in at us. They would clank the bars of the jail cell. It seemed like an eternity.

"Finally my father came. He said, 'Get into the car.' We were just sick at our stomach and said, 'Dad, why didn't they call you? You must have been worried sick about us.'

"Dad said they *had* called, and he had told them, 'Do you have a filthy cell to put them in? I want to scare them and set them straight.'

"The Law of Consequences was played out in our life. We were horrified. That's how my dad liked to articulate lessons in life, such as The Law of Consequences.

"My dad was the first Mr. Mom. My mom worked so hard over the years to be able to support the family and all of Dad's goals. Dad would take us to our doctor's appointments. He took some of us to get our first bra. We were going to a church youth event, and I needed a bathing suit. Of course Mom was very modest and wanted her daughters to be modest, and I was looking at one-piece bathing suits that came up to my neck. Dad got me aside and said, 'Come over here. All the kids are wearing these bathing suits, a two-piece' (not a bikini). He got me a two-piece pink-and-white checked swimsuit. I thought I was one of the gang now! It was hard for us to be in Africa and then come back to the States and try to adjust to this culture. My dad was the first Mr. Mom of the Universe.

"Preaching is a big job. It is not just standing in the pulpit. It is taking care of people' needs, counseling, teaching Bible classes, and much more.

Churches have many issues and problems, so Dad once decided to sell Pepperidge Farm Bread. It didn't last long, because it was not God's plan. Pretty soon Dad realized that we needed more income, so Dad, Mom, and John sold fresh ground corn meal and hush puppies over the week-ends."

Cathy went to the pulpit again.

"As Jan mentioned, there would be times when problems arose with philosophy or with elders and deacons. Other times Dad just needed a break. Dad is a multi-talented person, and the gift he gave us children was that there is nothing you cannot do. He had convinced us that we could even be brain surgeons or astronauts. He would go off on these deviations once in a while. He sold furniture, and he sold insurance, and he sold cars. All of these little deviations were short-lived because Dad was not very successful in any of them. He always went back to preaching, because that was his first love. His heart was in preaching. In these deviations Dad changed. He wasn't the same Dad that we were used to, and we were always glad when he went back to preaching. We welcomed him back.

"He loved to build. He built furniture, houses, churches."

Pictures of our sunroom came onto the screen, and Cathy talked about them. "This picture shows what the back of the house looked like before the sunroom was built when Mom and Dad first bought the house fifteen or so years ago. My mom, bless her heart! She worked so hard through the years to support Dad's goals. The back of the house looked pretty bleak, but Dad convinced Mom that he could build a sunroom—even though that might mean that Mom would need to get a second job to pay for it. No project was too big. On a road-block he would always say, 'Let's pray about it!' He knew that God would always come through.

"My dad was one of the most industrious men I have ever met. He had so many projects going, and they always went along so well. He taught us a work ethic that is important now, and we are passing that along to our own children. Dad spent years building the sunroom where he died. When Mom and Dad had bought the house, it was in need of major repairs. Attached to the back of the house was a rundown wooden deck. Dad was so pleased when he had completed the sunroom. Dad was so passionate about family reunions, and when we all came, we brought chainsaws and work clothes. Dad was not a talker, but a doer. We all joined on the work parties that he planned."

Debbie now went to the pulpit again and said, "Dad always had a lot of sayings. When we complained, he said, 'Make your words tender and sweet, for those are the very ones you will have to eat.' When we faced challenges, he would say, 'That's between you and God.' When we were worried, 'Let's cross that bridge when we get there.' When we were frustrated with a project that wasn't going perfectly, 'I like the way you did it better than the way they didn't.' And lastly, 'I don't believe in luck. I believe in God's purpose.'"

At his seventy-fifth birthday party, Harold had said that each of our family was a unique snowflake. Now I was thrilled to see these snowflakes bonding together into a team to present the many facets of Harold's personality. I was surprised and pleased with the honesty and love with which they shared their memories.

When the stories had all been told, Diana went to the pulpit and said, "A few weeks ago Dad taught his last lesson from John 14 from his hospital bed in the sunroom. We were all hanging on every word wondering what he would say—what great pearls of wisdom. There was a long pregnant pause. Then Dad suddenly burst out singing, "What the world needs now is love, sweet love."

The girls all rose and stood together and sang.

"What the world needs now is love sweet love. That's the only thing there's just too little of. What the world needs now is love sweet love."

The next picture etched in my memory was the long line of people walking past the open casket. I sat in the front row by the casket, a flood of tears streaming down my cheeks. But even as I felt my mind becoming numb, I could feel the warmth of friends and family as they reassured me with their warm hugs and tender words of compassion.

Chapter 5
Where Are You, God?

For this is God, our God forever and ever; He will be our guide even to death.
—Psalm 48:14 (NJKV)

After the funeral some of our family stayed to visit and to help me get the house in order. One evening one of our granddaughters, Helene, who has always lived many miles away from us in Collierville, Tennessee, took me aside.

"Grandma," she said, "who was Grandpa? I really missed knowing him," she slowly asked. "Would you tell me how it all began? How did you meet Grandpa? How did you know you would marry him?"

"Let's go out on the front porch and sit in the swing and talk," I said. "Are you ready to hear? It's a long story."

"Grandma, I would love to hear!" she said, and she sat by me in the swing.

"The story is all about God answering my prayers," I replied, "and giving me my soul mate."

My thoughts drifted back—way back, and I told Helene the story.

I had been introduced to death very early in life. Two years before I was born, and two months after Mother and Daddy were married, my paternal grandparents had both died in the great flu pandemic of 1930. They left three children. My parents took in the two girls, Ella Mae and Ruby. Ella Mae was a bright-eyed, affectionate ten-year-old girl with a sunny disposition. At eleven she developed a heart malfunction that made her an invalid for the rest of her brief life. Ruby was a shy, bewildered, eight-year-old girl, stunned by the loss of both parents. She was very close to her sister, Ella Mae.

My brother Jack was born the January that I turned two. Jack only weighed five pounds when he was born. He was frail, cried often, and demanded a lot of attention. Mother had been in poor health her entire second pregnancy, and she was unable to care for me without assistance. Ella Mae adored me and insisted that she was able to care for me on her bed. She spent entire days pampering, coddling, and spoiling me. I eagerly coveted her gentleness and affection.

After bravely fighting a two-year battle with her incurable illness, Ella Mae passed from this life at the age of thirteen. The ugly fangs of death left a trail of ghastly reminders. Weeping. Sobbing. Mourning. Loneliness. Silence. One evening at home, weeks after the funeral, and after outward signs of mourning had ceased, supper was ready, and little Ruby was gone! Mother and Daddy searched until they found her hiding in the back corner of a dark closet, crying softly.

The thought of death terrified me.

When I was old enough to read, I would hide books under my pillow at night, and when everyone had gone to sleep, I would turn on the night light and read. Very soon I discovered the Bible and spent hours pondering what it meant. I enjoyed discovering the exciting adventures of the Bible characters. My favorite character was David. I loved his poems in the Book of Psalms. David helped me to consider that God was a God of love.

Every time the Bible, church, or God were mentioned, our home became a battleground. Mother would plead with Daddy to go to church with us, but he would become angry, and Mother would end up in tears. Maybe Daddy was angry with God, and felt that God had robbed him of schooling that would enable him to have a job with shorter hours. He was an ambitious, hard-working man. With just an eighth-grade education he had moved up to manager of a large bakery with over seventy-five employees. I do not really know the reasons, but thoughts of religion aroused in him angry confrontations with whoever was available at the time. Usually this was Mother.

Daddy's furor did not dampen Mother's zeal for Christ. Every Sunday morning, Ruby, Jack, and I traveled to church on the bus. After an hour of waiting, riding, waiting, and riding, we reached the north side of the Indiana town where we lived. From the bus stop we walked several blocks more to a small, white, frame church building. Rain, snow, or sunshine, we attended church every Sunday morning.

The preacher was an older man who used charts and blackboard sermons. Usually he ended his lengthy sermons with loud, vehement descriptions of the fires of Hell. I was baptized when I was ten. I thought about Daddy—and the battleground at home—and I started praying that God would let me be the wife of a preacher some day. I wanted a husband who really knew God like King David did and who really knew that God was a God of love.

After seventeen years, the power of the gospel won out: Daddy surrendered his life to Christ, and he was immersed in baptism. The regrets of his early rebellion to the Word of God spurred him to become a greater, more useful servant of Christ. Daddy was a dynamic soul winner, and the year before Mother died, he held home Bible studies several evenings a week and baptized over one hundred people. Mother was so thankful that when she was too feeble to go out, she invited people into their home so she could continue to be a part of Daddy's great work.

When I was fifteen, I dated an assorted variety of young men in my high school class, but no one young man was really special to me. I kept looking and hoping that someday God would answer my prayers and send along someone who wanted to become a preacher and who really knew God.

I met Harold for the first time on a city bus. In those days the only way to get to school was to take public transportation, walk, or have your dad drive you to school on his way to work. I lived two miles from the high school in the center of town. In warm weather, I would walk to school with some of my classmates, but in winter I would ride the city bus. Usually the bus was crowded, and I had to stand up.

A young man about eighteen years old with black curly hair and smiling brown eyes always sat in the back of the bus with his girl friend.

One morning he was on the bus and there was no longer any girl friend. His eyes met mine, and I smiled and blushed. Quickly I looked away, but I felt he was still staring at me. Just then the bus jolted to a quick stop, and I lost my balance and dropped my books. As I stooped down to pick up my scattered papers and books, he got up from his seat and stooped down.

"Let me help you," he said.

"Thank you," I said, blushing.

"May I take you to the basketball game Friday night?"

"Yes."

"I'll see you at seven. I know where you live. I live across the street in the next block."

On our first date, he forgot his billfold and only realized it as we were standing in line for tickets. On our second date, the car stalled. It was twenty degrees below zero and snowy. This was the beginning of a whole chain of exciting and unforgettable incidents. Our romance progressed quickly. Sledding adventures on snow covered hills. Basketball games. Football games. Symphony concerts. Thursday night suppers with his large extended family. All of these events were interspersed with long, deep conversations when we came home. We always sat on the couch in the living room and talked for hours about our dreams and visions for the future, our disappointments and failures, our home life and families, and the way we were raised.

"When I get married," Harold said, "I want to have a big family. I want twelve boys and then I can have my own football team. It was lonely being raised with just one brother, and one who was five years older at that. He never wanted me around. One time he locked me up in the chicken house. I can still hear those chickens clucking and feel them pecking on me."

Although Harold only had one brother, he had dozens of aunts, uncles, and cousins, and they were loving and closely knit. His mother was the youngest of seven children, and although her parents were dead, her siblings all lived nearby, and they kept in close contact with each other. They met every Thursday evening at the Saddle Club to eat and play cards. Sometimes as many as fifty people came. They laughed and joked, and sometimes the parties turned into a big square dance.

By the end of summer it was evident that our romance was progressing swiftly. But I was perplexed. I knew that I was beginning to love Harold very much, but never would he be the preacher I dreamed of marrying—so I thought at the time. In our long conversations we rarely spoke about God, religion, or the church. He knew that I attended church, but seemed uncomfortable whenever I mentioned it or suggested that he take me sometime. When I thought about the possibility of maybe sometime marrying Harold, I was in a quandary.

Many times I prayed that God would open up Harold's heart to the Word of God, as he had Daddy's. At Thanksgiving the unpredictable Indiana weather turned bitterly cold. Freezing rain mixed with snow greeted us every morning. The biting winds blistered our cheeks as we walked to the bus. Harold got a deep cough that suddenly turned into viral pneumonia. Before I knew it, he had taken a turn for the worse. From my upstairs bedroom window I could see his uncle, Doctor Forsyth, visit him twice a day. Harold's mother suggested I not come to visit, because his condition was critical and he might not make it through the night.

In despair, I ran to my room, threw myself on my Jenny Lind twin bed, sobbed into my pillow, and prayed.

"Dear God, please spare Harold's life! I love him so much. Please heal him! Please cause him to love me as deeply as I love him. If you do, Dear God, I promise to serve you, and to have a Christian home for you. Please heal him!"

Then I drifted into sleep.

The days turned into weeks, and the weeks turned into months before I saw any indication that God was answering my prayers. In the spring Harold had recovered enough to be out, and he sometimes came over to chat for a few minutes. But he acted like a stranger to me. We did not have long conversations any more as we sat on the couch or the porch swing. We just had long silences and talk of the weather and trivialities.

Then one warm summer evening as we sat in the swing enjoying the fragrance of the honeysuckle and watching the lightning bugs twinkle in the dark, Harold turned to me and announced, "Jane Ann, as you know, I had to drop out of college when I was sick. Aunt Juanita told me that I am going to be drafted very soon. She has a friend who saw the roster. I'm going to be drafted, so I—"

"How can they draft you!" I interrupted. "Aren't you enrolled for college this fall?"

"Yes, but that doesn't matter."

"Doesn't matter!"

"No, I would be drafted anyway. So I enlisted in the Air Force today."

"You, what?"

"You heard me. I enlisted in the Air Force today!"

"When do you leave?"

"I leave August 25. So we still have a few days together before I leave."

I tried hard to choke back the tears.

"Will you miss me?"

"Of course, I'll miss you, funny face," he said. He pulled me closer and kissed me tenderly.

"Will you write to me?"

"Yes, I'll write."

Before I knew it, the days had flown by, and I was giving Harold a going-away present. I gave him a Bible, and *Hurlbut's Story of the Bible,* and a box of stationery. By this time the Korean War was raging, and I had grave doubts when and if we would ever meet again. But I prayed!

In the months ahead I never realized the beautiful and unusual way that God was answering my prayers. Harold was assigned to Keesler Air Force at Biloxi, Mississippi. And yet I complained a lot and cried often. I spent my days writing letters to Harold. I just lived from one day's mail delivery to the next.

Before I knew it, our letters were discussing God. Harold had been reading the Bible every day and was halfway through the New Testament. When I read his letters, I detected an excitement about the new discoveries he had made in his reading. Some of his zeal made me ashamed that I had not been bolder in discussing the Bible with him sooner.

One day he wrote me that he was convinced that he needed to be baptized. He had read the Book of Acts two times and was explaining to me what it said.

"Did you know all of these things were in the Bible?" he wrote. "Why did you not tell me sooner?"

I felt my face flush with embarrassment. Why hadn't I mentioned my concern for his soul sooner? Why hadn't I made more effort to communicate to him things that I had really taken for granted? I had gone to church since I was a small child and had heard these things many times.

My feelings of uncertainty now went away. As the long weeks and months passed, as our letters became more intimate, as I missed him more and more, as I prayed for him every day, I realized deeply in my heart that Harold was the one I wanted to marry.

The time passed by, and we decided to get married. Harold would get a ten-day leave, and his parents would drive to Biloxi and bring him home to Indiana for the wedding. Little did I know the challenges we would face as we moved ahead with our plans. The first barrier was legal. We were both too young to marry without the written consent of our parents. Harold was the youngest in his family, and if he married, his parents would face an empty nest. In time, however, they gave their consent. My daddy, on the other hand, took a lot of convincing. But Mother and I prayed, and he finally signed, too.

Harold's mother, Susie, was a strong, independent, take-charge woman. She had a car, and she wasn't afraid to drive it anywhere. My mother could not drive. So almost immediately Susie took charge of our wedding plans.

"If this is going to happen," Susie said, "then it will be the best wedding ever. We must have imported holly from England for the floral arrangements.—Let's go shopping, Janie. We need to pick out your wedding rings. You can have any you want.—I know you are busy typing the invitations and going to school and are having a difficult time sewing your wedding gown. Let's go to Aunt Gail's tomorrow, and she will hem it for you."

Then another complication arose. Harold wrote that I must send a letter to his commanding officer and request permission to get married. After many anxious moments and many prayers, this is what I wrote:

Miss Jane Ann Critchlow
Terre Haute, Indiana
November 4, 1950

To the Commanding Officer of
Private Harold L. Derr

I am praying that you will read my letter. Harold told me that you discouraged us getting married. Maybe you did not understand the circumstances. You must be thinking of all of the broken hearts in the past war. Probably if you analyzed the lives of most of those people, they weren't living right in the sight of God before they were married.

Harold and I have been dating for about two years. He lives across the street from me. He is a very outstanding person. He doesn't smoke, or drink, or gamble, or do many other worldly things such as that, so why wouldn't our marriage be a success?

Before we are married he is going to be baptized, then we shall both be of the same faith, the Church of Christ.

We realize that we won't have a big bank account to start on, but we both feel that through our love for each other and our faith in God, we will never be wanting. As long as we try to please God, why wouldn't God watch over and protect us?

In March I will be a graduate of Terre Haute Commercial College, and will then be able to meet the expenses that will come.

We thought that it was just formality to ask your permission and now our parents and I have practically completed the wedding plans. So it would be a tragedy if you denied us your permission.

If God is willing, may you grant our request.
Cordially yours,
Jane Ann Critchlow

While I waited anxiously for the commanding officer to reply, Susie kept me busy with wedding arrangements. Mother arranged for our preacher, Doyle Earwood, to perform the ceremony and to arrange for Harold's baptism. The wedding would be the first in the new church building. Mother also arranged for a forty-member *a cappella* chorus to provide the music.

Susie arranged our honeymoon. Harold's older brother Gene was married to Rosemary. They lived an hour's drive away in a small town. They would remain in Terre Haute after the wedding, and Harold and I would spend two or three days in their home alone.

The Saturday before the wedding was filled with activity. Harold and his parents arrived late because the roads had been covered with snow. Harold needed to sign papers for the county recorder, but the office was closed for the weekend. Susie took care of it: we went to the recorder's home and signed. Mother, Daddy, Jack, and Ruby were busy preparing our home for the reception after the wedding Sunday afternoon, and arranging for the photographer to come there as well as to the church.

After a tense day all of us in the wedding party arrived at the church for the rehearsal. Some of Harold's curious aunts and uncles came, too. The rehearsal went well. After the preacher prompted his ten-year-old daughter and the other children in the wedding one more time how to perform, he asked everyone to quietly find a seat in the front and to remain seated. Harold was going to confess Christ and be baptized.

As the wedding party moved to the front to sit down, I saw that several of Harold's family were leaving. I sat at the end of the pew, stunned. I could hear my heart pounding. Then Harold's Aunt Alice came and put her arms around me.

"I am very proud of you," she said. "Your influence has changed Harold greatly." Her eyes filled with tears. "I wish I had done that years ago before I got married."

I took a deep breath as Alice got up and moved toward the back. I could see that Harold's parents and Gene and Rosemary had already left the building. I wondered how this would affect the wedding day, our honeymoon, and Harold's plans to get back to the base.

But I hardly had time to think about it, for now Harold was standing very tall and saying to the audience and to the preacher, "I believe that Jesus is the Messiah, the Son of God, that he died on the cross, and that God resurrected him on the third day."

In a few moments the baptistery drapes opened, and we heard the swishing of the water as Harold and the preacher stepped in.

The preacher raised his hand and said, "I baptize you in the name of the Father, the Son Jesus the Christ, and the Holy Spirit, for the remission of your sins, and that you might receive the gift of the Holy Spirit."

Much later that night, Harold and I sat on the couch in my parents' living room, talking over the events of the evening. Harold told me how happy and relieved he was after his baptism. He told me that when his unit was being transported to Biloxi, they had missed the plane at O'Hare Field in Chicago. The plane had crashed, and everyone aboard had been killed. He told of another narrow escape when he had gone by train to Texas for basic training. Then he said again how relieved he was that God spared his life so he could be baptized.

Then our conversation turned to laughter. We wondered if the children would be able to walk down the aisle and not drop the rings or trip on the train of my wedding gown or drop the basket of flowers!

Next morning, on that Christmas Eve Sunday in 1950, I jumped out of bed and looked out the window. I was seventeen, and this was my wedding day! The sun shone through the icicles on the sycamore trees. Everything was covered with large glistening snowflakes. They sparkled like diamonds in the early morning sunlight.

"Breakfast is ready," Mother called from downstairs.

After breakfast, when everyone else had left the room except Mother and I, I realized that from now on everything would change. I would shortly have a home of my own. Sensing my uneasiness, Mother stopped her dishwashing and sat down at the table with me. She reached over and took my hand.

"I love you," she said.

Just then the front door bell rang. We could hear Daddy talking to someone, and we listened.

"Oh, no! Why didn't you call us sooner?"

"Carol kept thinking that she would be well by today, and she really wanted to be in the wedding."

One of my bridesmaids had come down with the measles and couldn't be in the wedding. Now I must find someone to fit into her dress. Before I knew it the entire household was in a frenzy trying to help me solve the problem in a hurry. Daddy went over to Carol's house to try to bargain to get the dress. Carol was angry and didn't want anyone else to wear it. I knew my wedding would be spoiled!

Mother, in her I-know-that-everything-is-going-to-be-all-right tone of voice said, "Jane Ann, is it all right if I call Harold's sister-in-law Rosemary? I think she and Carol are about the same size, and she is coming to the wedding anyhow."

"You can try," I said reluctantly.

Just then the door slammed and Daddy rushed inside. He dropped a large box on the couch.

"Jane Ann, you'd better hang this dress up right away before it gets wrinkled."

"Oh, Daddy, thank you!" I said and ran and threw my arms around him and gave him a big hug and kiss.

Mother entered the room smiling and announced that Rosemary was coming over in a few minutes to pick up the dress, and that she would be happy to be in the wedding. Everything was going to be all right after all.

After his leave was over, Harold returned to the base without me. I had to wait until my first allotment check came for us to have enough money to live together.

We were so much in love that it didn't matter to us that we were very young and very poor. Our love for each other and our desire to be together overshadowed everything else. If God had revealed to us at that time that we would make our home in thirty-two different houses over fifty-five years and would still be living from one "allotment check" to the next, we would still have made the same decision. For in no other way could God have proved to us his great promise: "Don't be anxious about tomorrow. God will take care of your tomorrow too. Live one day at a time."

"Grandma," Helene whispered softly. "Do you think that God will take care of you now?"

I sat in silence. The sun had gone down, and the evening darkness was upon us.

"I can't believe that we have been here talking this long!" I said. "Let's go inside and see what the others are doing. We can talk again later."

My voice trailed off as I opened the front door and went inside.

Helene followed in silence.

As the children and grandchildren said their goodbyes one by one and went home, as the noise of the great-grandchildren running down the hall stopped, as I sat in the recliner not far from where Harold had died, I was alone. Although it had only been a week since the funeral, the memory of it all was a blur. Everything was quiet. The silence was deafening.

I took a deep breath and thought about the conversation with Helene in the porch swing. Did I really believe that God would take care of me? I had not answered her.

I picked up my Bible from the table nearby and opened it. My eyes were drawn to this passage: "For God has not given us a spirit of fear, but of power and of love and of a sound mind" (2 Tim. 1:7 NKJV). As I pondered this, I remembered the strength it had given me many years ago at a time when I was frightened.

My thoughts went back in time to the mid 60s, when we had just returned from Ghana. Why was I thinking about that? I was curious to know, so I sorted through my old journals. This is what I found.

Late August, 1965. Since we came back from Ghana, I am facing a dilemma: the only way we can survive financially with five growing children ages seven to fourteen is for me to get a job. The scary thing for me is confronting any prospective employer with my stuttering problem and my lack of job skills. When I think of the paralyzing fear that sometimes completely blocks my speech, I begin to feel helpless. My face burns red hot with embarrassment as I watch listeners look away in disgust. I can feel the gnawing pain eating away in my soul.

So I pray, and afterwards I feel my mind changing directions, and I remember the delight I always feel when I listen to Harold preach and teach. He has the gift of making Bible characters come alive. Afterwards he shows how God and Jesus Christ are alive today. God will help us in the same ways that he helped people in Bible times.

My thoughts turn to our immediate challenges. I cannot let Harold and the children down. We are so content with our life in Quartz Hill, California. The people have accepted us into their hearts as family. We have been blessed by their love and kindness. It was important to us after coming back from our volatile missionary experiences in Ghana, where we faced many extraordinary obstacles that tested our faith to the utmost.

But in Ghana, we faced these challenges together. That made all the difference. Now I must branch out on my own. How can I do it?

Early September, 1965. I have decided to put the promise of 2 Timothy 1:7 to the test: "For God has not given us a spirit of fear, but of power and of love and a sound mind." I have prayed and then set out on a job search. Praying, seeking, and looking turned up three employment opportunities: a sales clerk in a department store, an office job at a car dealership, and a job as postal clerk in a town forty miles away.

The job as sales clerk job was only part-time. But the office job was fulltime, so I accepted. It was a baby step to a new adventure on my solo journey with God.

Not long after I started, we received a report that Harold's dad in Indiana was in critical condition and not expected to live many more days. After prayer, we determined that Harold would drive the children to

Indiana to spend time with their grandpa, and I would stay in California and finance the trip.

The family left for Indiana, and I traveled to work praying for a good day. Shortly after my arrival, I was told that the receptionist had called in sick, and my job would be to handle the calls that came in through the telephone switchboard. The telephone system was massive, and the harder I tried to master it, the more difficult it was for me. Callers had trouble understanding me. I had problems transferring calls. When the chairman of the board called in from another state, I unsuccessfully transferred his calls twice and disconnected them both times.

I was fired. I drove home trembling. What now?

As I turned the key to open the door at home, I heard the telephone ringing. I rushed to pick up the receiver.

"Are you Jane Ann Derr?" The voice was loud and booming.

"Yes, I am," I answered slowly.

"I'm Ray Daniels from the Post Office. A postal clerk job just opened up at our sectional center in Mojave. Are you able to report for work tomorrow night at six?"

My heart pounded "Yes!" I blurted out. "I'll be there!"

That was yesterday, and last night I rolled and tossed in bed wondering what challenges would be waiting for me on my first day at work. I fear driving the forty miles alone tonight, because Harold is still in Indiana. I wonder if I am strong enough to handle the 125-pound mail sacks. My days of housework and office work haven't qualified me for this type of work. Harold has always done the heavy housework like mopping and vacuuming. He even makes sure my car is always running properly, and he keeps the gas tank filled.

So last night I decided to tell myself, "God has not given us a spirit of fear, but of power and of love and of a sound mind." Then I closed my eyes and prayed. I bundled up my fears in little balloons and released them to God. I opened my Bible and read, "It is vain for you to rise up early, to sit up late; to eat the bread of sorrows; for so He gives His beloved sleep" (Ps. 127:2).

The sound of three young deer running across the back yard brought me back to the here and now. I closed the journal from so many years before, took a deep breath, and looked around. The leaves were crimson and gold. The sky was a deep blue with a few white fluffy clouds.

I got up from the recliner and started clearing out the closets. I telephoned the Viet Nam Veterans and scheduled a pick-up date. It was not a day for a spirit of fear.

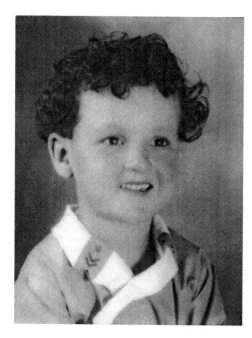

Harold Derr,
age five.

Jane Ann
Critchlow,
age seven,
and brother
Jack, age
five.

Harold and Jane Ann in the Critchlow living room before the Wiley High School Sweetheart Dance. Harold built the model ship on the bookcase. 1949.

Harold enlisted in the Air Force in August 1950. This picture was made the following October.

Harold and Jane Ann cutting their wedding cake, December 24, 1950.

Family group on wedding day. Jane Ann and her parents, Loran and Luetta Critchlow, are to the left, Harold and his parents, Tonie and Susie Derr, are to the right.

Harold with Debbie in Biloxi, Mississippi, December 1951.

Family in Waco, Texas. From l. to r.: Jane Ann, Diana, Debbie (standing), Harold. 1953.

Family in Desert Lake, California, 1957. From l. to r.: Jane Ann, Janice, Debbie, Diana, Cathy, and Harold.

Family in Desert Lake, California, 1959. From l. to r.: Janice, Jane Ann, Debbie (standing), John, Harold, Cathy, Diana.

Church group, Obuasi, Ghana, West Africa. Jane Ann and Harold and some others are wearing the traditional kente. 1965.

Children wearing crowns at vacation Bible school, Suminakese, Ghana, West Africa. Summer 1965.

Harold and Dewayne Davenport in front of the church building in Suminakese after Sunday worship. 1963.

Harold treating a wound on a Ghanaian boy from the back of the Volkswagen bus after a village worship service. 1964.

Family in Fresno, California, when Harold preached at the Arlington Heights Church. First row, l. to r.: Jane Ann, John, Cathy, Harold; second row, l. to r.: Janice, Diana, Debbie. 1968.

Family in the home of Jane Ann's parents in San Diego. On floor, l. to r.: John, Cathy; seated, l. to r.: Diana, Debbie, Jane Ann, Janice, Harold. 1968.

The Derr family with Jane Ann's parents and Jane's Aunt Ruby in Quartz Hill, California. From l. to r.: Loran Critchlow, Ruby Critchlow, Luetta Critchlow, John, Jane Ann, Cathy, Janice, Debbie, Diana, Harold. 1966.

Jane Ann and her grandchildren around the oak table in Atlanta. From l. to r.: Jane Ann, Shauna Ashcraft, Amanda Ashcraft, Diana (hidden), and Jason Ashcraft. Christmas, 1985.

Harold the builder. He enjoyed the journey as much as the destination. On this page he is shown at work on the sunroom of his house in Cumming, Georgia, in the late 1990s.

A table that Harold designed and built from recycled materials: marble from the old Dodgers Stadium in Los Angeles and wood from an old church building.

Harold at the Etowah River Church of Christ, Dawsonville, Georgia, as it was under construction in early 2000.

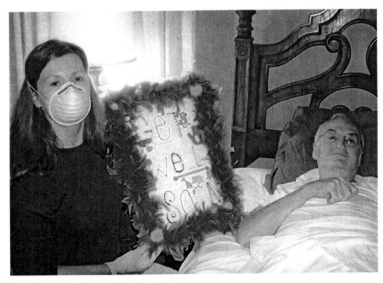

Debbie showing Harold a get-well card made by his grand-daughters Helene and Rachelle Lagotte. The mask protects Harold's weakened immune system. 2006.

Janice and Harold, shortly after he had fallen. 2006.

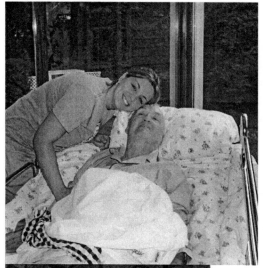

A visitor from church, Kim Foster, with Harold in the sun room.

Harold with Asa Frakes's cane.

Family group with Harold and Jane Ann and their children and grandchildren, 1998.

Harold and Jane Ann while Harold was minister of the Etowah River Church.

Part 2

Chapter 6
The Beauty of Solitude

Be still, and know that I am God; I will be exalted among the nations, I will be exalted in the earth.
—Psalm 46:10

As the funeral, the burial, and the kindnesses of friends gradually become history, you move into the stage in which you will spend the rest of your life: the long-term processing of your grief. This stage bears a remarkable resemblance to the second and third day following major surgery. The anesthesia begins to wear off and you begin to realize just how much the wound really hurts.

In the Creator's wisdom, our minds are designed to go into shock when a loved one dies. Our circuits blow. When there are things too awful to be considered, the brain mercifully lets them pass through without seriously processing them. In the coming years, you will probably look back on what you are going through today and realize that—even when you thought you were right on top of things—your mind was on hold.
—Charlie Walton, *When There Are No Words*

As I look back after traveling three and a half years down the journey of grief, Charlie Walton's

words quoted above really speak to my heart. Yes,
God does blot out of our mind the events that were
too awful to be considered.

After many attempts through the years—attempts
that ended in failure, that ended in gut-wrenching
tears, that ended in sleepless nights—I was able to
view the video that had been made of Harold's
funeral. As I listened carefully, as I watched intently,
I realized for the first time that God had blocked out
of my mind the dark moments I was unable to
comprehend. When life events take your breath
away, it takes time to catch your breath.

The journey through grief is a time of
remembering, reflecting, and processing the past
from a new perspective. The way you process
memories now depends on how you have viewed God
in the past. Thoughts of the Holy One are life-seeds
planted. If these seeds have been precious to you,
and if you have cared for them daily by listening to
God's Word and praying for discernment, when trials
come you will know what to do in crisis. There is
great security in relying on the power of reading
God's Word and getting down on your knees in
prayer.

One morning after I finished my prayers, I
remained, waiting and listening for what God might
say to me. In a few moments, a picture came dancing
into my mind: I saw file cabinet drawers full of note
pads with only one or two sheets in each. I started
thinking, why do I get a new note pad before I use up
the old one? I laughed, thinking, "What does this

have to do with my spiritual journey? That's a crazy idea."

The picture however hung around to haunt me, and I wondered what it meant.

Before long I was thinking about the layers of this crazy habit of mine. I remembered something that Harold kept repeating to me.

"Jane Ann," he would say, "you always bite off more than you can chew!"

Of course I had always denied it. But now I could feel the sting prick my heart as I faced certain flawed habits of mine: multi-tasking, ever shortening attention span, over-commitment to church and family activities, entrapment in extensive research loops and only skimming the surface, distraction by new information, becoming overwhelmed with new activities.

A few days later these thoughts were still bothering me, and I prayed for answers. I wondered whether this meant that I lacked the ability to finish what I had started. Then I remembered Harold's constant prayer, "When my work is finished, quickly take me home."

"What does all this mean?" I wondered. "Does it mean that I am afraid to die?"

Emptiness of Death, Fullness of Hope

Several weeks later, I discovered a sermon that Harold had preached on April 15, 1979. The sermon showed that even emptiness—for me especially now the emptiness of death and loss—can be seen in a positive way. Our fear of death and its emptiness can be lessened, or even removed, as it was for Harold, by the fullness of hope. This is what I read:

This week I was eating lunch at Hardee's and saw a young mother bring in her two children. The little boy, about five years old, sat in the booth waiting for his mother to go through the line and get his lunch. His eyes sparkled and his face had the radiance of expectation. He watched every move his mother made as she went through the line. In a moment she brought the food back, and he sat patiently as she distributed the food to the children. At the prescribed time, the little boy knew that he had to make a decision. Was he going to eat a French fry first or a bite of his sandwich, or was he going to take a big drink of the soda? Finally, the French fries won out. So he sat enjoying his selection. His face radiated the excitement of enjoying his French fries. After a short while, the fries were all gone. Now I watched him take the sack and very carefully tear it to each corner, in anticipation that some little goodie might have lodged there. It wasn't long until the sandwich was gone—and he had learned to pick up the sesame seeds. He meticulously picked them all up and ate them. Finally he leaned back in his seat, put the soda straw to his lips, and took a long draw. He took the second. All of a sudden that sound came that all of us are familiar with. I watched. By this time, it was beautiful. He removed the little plastic lid, took the straw, and carefully parted all of the ice in the cup. He put the very tip of the straw right down in the uttermost bottom and he slurped again. It was all gone. He set the cup back on the table and looked around, and I noticed by this time the expression on his face had faded. Then, as if thinking, "I'll try it again," he reached for the cup and gave it one more s-l-u-r-p. But the old sound was not there, and he set the cup down. The sparkle from his eyes was now gone. The expectation had faded. The expression on his face changed. Empty! This just seems to be so depressing and sad today in our culture.

In contrast, the Apostle John saw that the word "empty" was invigorating, was exciting, and he carried this theme throughout his entire Gospel. His three themes were: an empty cross, an empty tomb, and an empty mansion. To John, these three themes were beautiful and a part of his entire life. I would like to share them with you today.

The Empty Cross

"Just as Moses lifted up the snake in the wilderness, so the Son of Man must be lifted up, that everyone who believes in him may have eternal life in him. For God so loved the world that he gave his one and only Son, that whoever believes in him shall not perish but have eternal life" (John 3:14–16).

The Empty Tomb

"Jesus said to her, 'I am the resurrection and the life. He who believes in Me, though he may die, he shall live. And whoever lives and believes in Me shall never die. Do you believe this?' " (John 11:25–26 NKJV).

"Early on the first day of the week, while it was still dark, Mary Magdalene went to the tomb and saw that the stone had been removed from the entrance. So she came running to Simon Peter and the other disciple, the one Jesus loved, and said, 'They have taken the Lord out of the tomb, and we don't know where they have put him!' So Peter and the other disciple started for the tomb. Both were running, but the other disciple outran Peter and reached the tomb first. He bent over and looked in at the strips of linen lying there but did not go in. Then Simon Peter came along behind him and went straight into the tomb. He saw the strips of linen lying there, as well as the cloth that had been wrapped around Jesus' head. The cloth was still lying in its place, separate from the linen. Finally the other disciple, who had reached the tomb first, also went inside. He saw and believed. (They still did not understand from Scripture that Jesus had to rise from the dead)" (John 20:1–9).

An Empty Mansion

"Do not let your hearts be troubled. Trust in God; trust also in me. In my Father's house are many rooms; if it were not so, I would have told you. I am going there to prepare a place for you. And if I go and prepare a place for you, I will come back and take you to be with me that you also may be where I am. You know the way to the place where I am going" (John 14:1–5).

Thomas and the Message of Life

A few days after finding Harold's sermon, I turned in my daily devotion to a study of the Apostle Thomas. I found that Thomas's initial reaction to the death of Jesus was transformed into a lifelong mission to preach the resurrection.

For the story of Thomas, I looked first to the Gospel of John. The great contrasts in this book were interesting to me. John is the only Gospel that tells the story of Thomas, and the only one who says,

> For God loved the world so much that he gave his only Son so that anyone who believes in him shall not perish but have eternal life. God did not send his Son into the world to condemn it, but to save it. There is no eternal doom awaiting those who trust him to save them. But those who don't trust him have already been tried and condemned for not believing in the only Son of God (John 3:16–18, TLB)

I sat a long time thinking about the stark contrast between eternal doom and eternal life and how John, inspired by the Holy Spirit, included the intricate details of the beautiful story of the Apostle Thomas.

Thomas had been with Jesus. He had listened to Jesus teach. He had watched him perform miracles and heal the sick, and he had watched Jesus die.

Afterward, at evening on the first day of the week, the other disciples met together. Thomas was not there. Jesus came, and he showed them his hands and his side, breathed on them, and gave them the Holy Spirit.

When the disciples later told Thomas what had happened, he refused to believe them. Why had Thomas avoided the other disciples? He had followed Christ for three years. He had been willing to go to Jerusalem and die with Christ. As he saw Jesus betrayed by Judas, as he saw him ridiculed and rejected by the crowds, beaten and whipped by the Roman soldiers, put to death in one of the cruelest deaths known to man—as he saw all this and knew of nothing he or his friends could do to stop it, Thomas became angry, maybe even bitter. He wanted to be alone to sulk. He felt bewildered and rejected and was unwilling to accept anything less than seeing for himself the print of the nails in Jesus' hands and putting his finger in the print of the nails and his hand in Jesus' side.

Thomas was honest about his feelings. He had the courage to face the way he felt. And he didn't live forever avoiding the other disciples. In a short time (eight days) he met with them again. Jesus appeared again, and this time Thomas was there. Jesus immediately spoke to him, but not with sharp criticism. Rather, Jesus met Thomas directly where Thomas was—a disturbed and confused man. He honored Thomas and addressed his immediate need.

The powerful result was that Thomas was the first person to say, "My Lord and my God!" He was the first to verbalize that Jesus was God and not just a great prophet.

Do you suppose some of the other disciples felt the same way, but were afraid to say it? Thomas wanted to admit his problem and confess it to others. Then the blessing came to him: Jesus the Christ healed his unbelief.

The Book of Acts tells us that Thomas lived on in Jerusalem as part of the Christian community. Apocryphal and other ancient literature contains conflicting stories about the death of Thomas, but all sources agree that he continued to serve Christ, preaching the good news. His adventures, his trials, and his missionary journeys are documented. Some say he died a natural death, whereas others say he was put to death by Misdai, the king of India. All agree, however, that Thomas preached the resurrection of Jesus Christ until his death.

Grief and the Heart

As a girl I watched my mother slowly separating the layers of an onion. In the same way, separating the layers of hidden emotions reveals the center of the heart, whether sweet or bitter, for all to see.

Peeling an onion makes me cry, and peeling away the layers of my hidden emotions also makes the tears flow. Why is that? Have we ever thought about it? How much time have we spent thinking about death—our own death?

We Americans do everything humanly possible to blot out thoughts of aging or death. Just look at the gross national sales of products that deceive us into thinking we will never age or die. In advertising we found breast augmentation, facial rejuvenation, lip enhancement, face lift, hair dye, buttocks enlargement, liposuction, natural wrinkle reduction, tummy tuck, image cosmetic surgery, laser hair removal, hair implant, and tattoo removal. We deny death and aging, and yet these conditions have lessons to teach us. Even the dying can change our lives.

Could the real problem be that we try to get over our grief by flatly refusing to think about our own death?

Take a few moments now and find a quiet spot to be completely alone. Close your eyes and imagine what thoughts would invade your mind if your doctor told you that you only had one week to live. What thoughts would rush in so quickly that your face would flush? How would you use the seven days?

Pain and Comfort

> Pain turns us to God. The value lies not in the pain itself, but in what we can make of it.
> —Philip Yancey, *Where Is God When It Hurts?*

After a period of intense work on this book, I developed a nagging pain in the left side of my chest. I ignored the pain for several weeks. Then one night the pain stressed me into an anxiety attack. I went on the internet to self-diagnose my problem, and the result was this: Go to the emergency room immediately!

Although it was quite late, I called Diana to take me. There I was rushed to tubes of oxygen, tubes for injections of medications, and other tubes for monitoring my heart. I was stunned at the recommendation that I should be admitted to the hospital for more tests. The next day a nurse woke me up early for a three-hour nuclear stress test, and afterward chest X-rays and blood samples. The hospital near us had been expanding for years, but I had no idea that so many diagnostic machines existed, and I think they used all of them on me.

Before and after the nuclear stress test I was required to lay very still on a cold stiff table for fifteen minutes. The minutes seemed to me like hours. During the test itself I was alone in a room with a machine monitoring my heart and blood vessels. While everything was very still except the movement of the machine passing over me, my mind began to fill with words from Psalm 139:

> For you created my inmost being; you knit me together in my mother's womb. I praise you because I am fearfully and wonderfully made; your works are wonderful, I know that full well. My frame was not hidden from you when I was made in the secret place, when I was woven together in the depths of the earth. Your eyes saw my unformed body; all the days ordained for me were written in your book before one of them came to be. How precious to me are your thoughts, God! How vast is the sum of them! Were I to count them, they would outnumber the grains of sand. (Ps. 139:12–18).

Then I felt that I was in the presence of God.

After many more tests, and many hours later, the doctor came into my room to tell me that my heart was very strong. He could find no problems at all. He suggested that the pain was due to acid reflux caused by stress. When I got home, I thanked God for his gracious care and asked for his help to turn all of my anxieties over to him. I thanked God for bringing the words of the psalm to my mind for comfort.

Waiting on God

After David had conquered Jerusalem, the Philistines spread out in the Valley of Rephaim. David inquired of God, and God told him to attack, and he would be with him. David obeyed and defeated them in the battle. Once more the Philistines came up and spread out in the Valley of Rephaim. This time, however, God said, "'Do not go straight up, but circle around behind them and attack them in front of the poplar trees. As soon as you hear the sound of marching in the tops of the poplar trees, move quickly, because that will mean the Lord has gone out in front of you to strike the Philistine army.' So David did as the Lord commanded him, and he struck down the Philistines all the way from Gibeon to Gezer" (2 Sam. 5:23-25).

After reading my daily devotional and praying, I decided that this was the time for me to wait and see what God has in store for my life.

I will lead the blind by ways they have not known, along unfamiliar paths I will guide them; I will turn the darkness into light before them and make the rough places smooth. These are the things I will do; I will not forsake them (Isa. 42:16).

Our daily moment-by-moment choices are like going to an eye doctor for an exam. As we look closely through a machine, he shows us two images and asks us to decide which one is clearer or which one is best. Sometimes it takes many attempts to decide which image is better. That's how moment-by-moment choices are. But God through the Holy Spirit reveals the clearer choice to us through prayer and the study of God's Word. We are on a life-time journey of moment-by-moment choices.

Releasing the Past

One day as I was cleaning out files trying to decide what to save and what to throw away, I found a journal that Harold had written in the mid 1950s. It came at a good time to help me to choose what to remember about the past and what to forget.

"Are not all angels ministering spirits sent to serve those who will inherit salvation?" (Heb. 1:14).

As a child I was constantly fascinated by a picture over the fireplace at my grandmother's house. Two little children walked across a swinging bridge. Lightning flashed in the black clouds, and the wind made the bridge swing. When I looked at this picture, my eyes were drawn to the beautiful angel behind the children, arms outstretched, ready to clasp them in case of danger.

Every time I read Hebrews 1:14 I think about this inspiring picture and wonder if I have entertained angels and never recognized them. Suddenly this scene popped into my head. It was 1956. I was preaching for a little church in Boron, California—right in the middle of the Mojave Desert. One Sunday evening when I stepped up to the pulpit, I noticed a crippled man walk in and take a seat in the back row. He was a stranger. As I continued preaching, I noticed how intently he listened, and how he lingered after the service was over and the others had left.

I went over to speak with him. I could feel the urgent need to listen as he spoke. He told me that he had been to a hospital in Los Angeles, and had been diagnosed with a terminal incurable illness. He was on his way home to Alaska. He intended to go home to die.

He avoided speaking about his illness or any of his needs except that he needed a ride to the crossroads—a little place called Four Corners—where he could get a trucker in an eighteen-wheeler to take him to Alaska. As we drove to Four Corners, he resumed his conversation about my need to continue preaching. He kept saying, "You must continue preaching and reach out to people and stay in the pulpit." He refused to talk about anything else except my steadfastness in preaching of Jesus the Christ.

All too soon we arrived at the little crossroads, and he got out of the car. I waited until he found a truck driver willing to take him. He came to the car and said that the truck was going to take him to Portland Oregon. He bid me goodbye and said, "God Bless".

As we drove home, I kept thinking about the stranger's words. His words kept rolling around in my mind. He had no way of knowing my thoughts, or my quandary. Just the week before, Jane Ann and I had had many long talks about the future. I was working seven days a week, getting little sleep, tired, and discouraged. I worked for the Air Force in the development of the engines for the Apollo Rocket. Things were not going well. It was a very demanding job. In addition I was trying to preach two sermons and teach two Bible classes every week, and trying to be a good husband and a good dad to our five children.

This stranger came for a moment and then vanished away. His words sank deep into my heart. Jane Ann and I were at the crossroads of a great decision at the time. We had spent many hours in prayer for God to direct our pathway. This stranger greatly influenced our choices. I resigned from the position at Edwards Air Force Base and chose to preach fulltime.

Had we entertained an angel?

After I read Harold's journal about his decision to preach fulltime, I remembered the encounter that our children and I experienced watching his last moments here on earth. He kept telling Janice about the beautiful sights he was seeing. He kept reaching his arms out as if he was trying to touch someone.

I wonder if an angel was standing behind his bed. I wonder what he saw.

After a time of remembering and reflecting, I decided that I must gently release the past to enjoy the now. I put the file in the back of the file cabinet. Perhaps the children will find it someday, I thought as I closed the drawer.

A godly person is like a tree planted by streams of water flowing from God. We are like a fragile leaf flowing gently down this stream. Like the leaf, as long as we allow God to gently glide us down the stream, we will arrive at the destination that God intends for us. However, if we, like the leaf, become entangled on a twig or a branch so we do not go forward, the rushing water will continue and we will be crushed by its impact. Like the rushing water, time waits for no one. We may desperately try to hang onto the rope of the past, and yet nothing will stay the same. Life is constantly moving on, and we must not become tangled up in a web that will destroy us. The past is an illusion. The now is real, and it is the path that leads us to a glorious future.

Chapter 7
The Rainbow after the Storm

Therefore, since we are surrounded by such a great cloud of witnesses, let us throw off everything that hinders and the sin that so easily entangles. And let us run with perseverance the race marked out for us, fixing our eyes on Jesus, the pioneer and perfecter of faith. For the joy set before him he endured the cross, scorning its shame, and sat down at the right hand of the throne of God.

—Hebrews 12:1-2

In the weeks and months that followed, I continued my morning prayers, anticipating that God would challenge my thoughts. Then one morning, to my surprise, my eyes seemed glued to the cane hanging on the headboard of my bed. It was the cane Harold had used when he could not stand alone. Many times I had held one of his arms, and he grasped the cane with his other hand.

My thoughts began to whirl as I remembered how I got the cane. The entire story was in a notebook in the file cabinet downstairs. I rushed downstairs to look for it.

My Mother's Diary

I wish now that I hadn't opened the file drawer, for right on the top of the notebook was Mother's diary and the little Bible she always carried in her purse. I reached in and pulled the diary out. I could still smell the faint fragrance of the perfume Mother always wore.

I opened the diary, and this is what I read:

February 28, 1977. This is a beautiful day.

Memories rushed in and sadness came over me. Mother had fought a five-year battle with multiple myeloma—and lost. She lost the battle, but she won the war. Her last words to me were, "Don't cry. Remember, this is the will of God. All things work together for good. Wait. You'll see!" She smiled, begged me not to cry, and fell asleep on March 30, 1977.

All during her long illness, her faith glowed, and she endured her afflictions with a smile. The people who came to cheer her up while she was bedfast always left feeling that Mother had cheered them up—and given them faith and hope as well. Over 150 people had visited and signed her guest book during the last month of her illness.

Why had they come?

In 1959 Mother and Daddy sold their little grocery store in Farmersburg Indiana, and moved to California to be nearer their grandchildren. They settled in San Diego, where Daddy found work. So at age fifty-three, they pulled up their roots and started all over again.

Very shortly after they moved, we were transferred back east.

For the next eighteen years, Mother and Daddy sought out lonely, forgotten people who had been discarded by the world, and they set out to bring sunshine into their lives. Daddy had never been a public speaker or teacher, but he started conducting home Bible studies using the Jule Miller filmstrips. For seventeen years, he and Mother held two or three classes each week, and the year before Mother passed away, Daddy baptized over one hundred people.

In addition to supporting Daddy in the Bible classes, Mother also taught a second grade Bible class. When she was too sick to go to church, the children walked across the church parking lot to her home. They would sit on the floor, and she would teach them from her bed. Mother always looked on her students as her own grandchildren and did many special things them. At her funeral, all of her pallbearers were students from her Bible classes.

Mother's greatest delight was to bring loveliness and joy into the lives of others. That is why she could always say, "This is a beautiful day."

I remembered all this and clutched Mother's diary to my breast and cried. Then I put the diary gently back into the file cabinet and continued my search for the story of Harold's cane.

I had come to get the story of Harold's cane, but I ended by uncovering other stories I had collected over the years. They had inspired me when I first read them, and I discovered I needed them more than ever now. My saints files.

The Story of the Cane

The cane had come to me as an answer to my prayers.

During Mother's long illness, I wanted desperately to know more about my ancestors.

After Harold and I were married, we moved constantly as his preaching assignments led us to Mississippi, Texas, Ohio, California, Indiana, Ghana West Africa, California, New Jersey, Kentucky, and North Carolina. While we were in North Carolina, Mother was having tremendous health problems. So I prayed a lot.

When we made our final trip to California to see Mother for the last time, as I was talking to Daddy in their apartment, he suddenly put a large box in my lap and asked me if I wanted it. The box contained the twenty-five-year genealogical searches of my great-aunt Etta Logan, whom I had last seen when I was five years old. I was amazed at the treasures inside. I was amazed how God had answered my prayers!

Back home in Winston-Salem, I spent hours sifting through the contents of the box. There were old letters and official papers. There was information that Aunt Etta had herself typed out. There were clippings from the *Terre Haute Tribune Star* and the *Sullivan Union*.

One document typed by Aunt Etta perked up my curiosity. My great-great-great grandfather, Asa Frakes, had been a Baptist preacher for thirty-eight years. What a pleasant surprise! I learned that he had been born in Nelson County, Kentucky, on April

10, 1803, and died in Prairie Creek Township, Indiana, December 8, 1873. When he was three years old he moved with his parents to Butler County, Ohio. His family lived there for three years, then moved to Franklin County, Indiana, and lived there until the fall of 1817. Then they moved to Prairie Creek Township. There Asa married Rebecca Dickerson, in February 1824, and in a short time bought the farm where he spent the rest of his life. He and Rebecca had ten children.

The newspaper clippings and my own internet searches filled in more details. Prairie Creek Township was east of the Wabash River. The first wagon road through the township was the old army road used for communication between Fort Knox and Fort Harrison during the War of 1812. The course of this road through the township was the only public highway in that part of the state up to 1823, when the present state road was laid out and opened.

For some years Prairie Creek bottom was the only way between the early settlements and the main army road. The bottom was open land at that time, and teamsters had no difficulty passing over it.

The first organized association formed in the township was the First Prairie Creek Baptist Church, constituted in May 1818 by Elder Isaac McCoy. Asa Frakes joined that church in May 1828 and was baptized into fellowship. Shortly after that, he appealed to Luke 4:8 and said that the spirit of the Lord was upon him, because he had been anointed to preach the gospel to the poor.

At that time Asa could neither read nor write, but with the help of Joel H. Kester he began to learn. People reported that they were amazed at his energy and powerful mind. He preached the word of God from Genesis to Revelation with a mastery that astonished his educated contemporaries. He was eloquent when fired with enthusiasm, and he was held to be one of the ablest preachers in the old Curry Association.

Asa and Rebecca raised ten children: four boys and six girls. In addition to his farm, he operated a pioneer grocery store across the road from the church. The store was made of logs and burned down in 1856. All the church records were stored there and were lost in the fire.

In the fashion of the day, Asa traveled far and near by horseback to preach the gospel. As he got older he was in poor health. He had a special chair built so he could preach sitting down, as he weighed 375 pounds. After a long period of suffering, he died on December 8, 1873. Near the door of the church that he served so faithfully, his grave is marked by an imposing monument that quotes 2 Timothy 4:7–8:

He has fought a good fight; he has finished his course; he has kept the faith; henceforth, there is laid up for him a crown of righteousness.

Shortly after I received Aunt Etta's box of family history, Harold was called to preach at the Friendly Avenue congregation, and we moved from Winston-Salem to Greensboro.

Several months after that, Aunt Etta's step-daughter found our new address, and she and her husband came to visit us. She brought a special gift for me—the cane that had belonged to my great-great-great grandfather Asa Frakes!

This was the cane that Harold used the month before he died, delivered to us by a couple I had never met. Luck? Coincidence? No. It was the providence of God answering my prayer. Yes, prayers are powerful and God listens to our hearts as we come to him in prayer.

Laura Long

As I continued my search in the file cabinet, I found a small file containing emails that Bill Long had sent out to friends and family when his wife Laura was dying with cancer. In the 1980s our family had attended the Sandy Springs Church of Christ (now known as North Atlanta). I remember Laura vividly as the person in the foyer who was constantly seeking out strangers and trying to make them feel welcome. She was a kind and gracious lady, loved by all who knew her. This is the story of Laura's last days and her passing.

Bill came to Sandy Springs in 1971 and served as pulpit minister until 1997. He has served as an elder since 1972 and is still serving. He helped lead the creation of the Genesis Center for Christian Counseling in the early 1990s. This is a part of a total family ministry that he began.

In July of 1998 Laura went to the doctor for a routine annual physical. Dr. Michael Sabom discovered a spot on her lung and directed her to have a biopsy. On July 10 Dr. Johnson did the biopsy and reported to Bill immediately after surgery that Laura had melanoma. Although they didn't fully understand the implications at first, Dr. Johnson told them that it was serious and that Bill should cancel his speaking engagements and give full attention to Laura.

The following emails tell the story.

October 20, 1998
Laura gets depressed at times and feels like giving up, but overcomes and continues to fight. Prayer and meditation help her a lot.

October 22, 1998
Laura's spirits are very good. She just accepts it as if that's the way it is; we'll just have to accept it. Her faith is so strong and she still is able to smile and there is not an inkling of anger. She does get depressed from time to time, but more over the pain and nausea than the prospect of a short life.

October 23, 1998
The doctor said, after looking more closely at the CT scans, that it is worse than he thought at first.

October 31, 1998
Laura has grown progressively weaker for the last few days . . . She is out of bed most of the day, but in her recliner a big portion of it . . . She has a wonderful spirit and though she would prefer otherwise, she is accepting what has come to her and trying to build more knowledge of and yearning for heaven. Not a bad idea for all of us. Please continue to pray for her to have some quality time left and even for God to heal, but that God's will be done and that he be glorified.

November 10, 1998

God has been very good to us. Laura said as we sat on the edge of the bed the other night praying, "God has been good to us." I still pray for God to heal her if it be his will, but pray for her comfort and for God to be in control and just lead us where he wants us to go. Thank you for your prayers.

November 17, 1998

It has been a very full day for Laura. I want to thank all of you for doing so much to help her have a happy birthday. She has received cards I know in excess of 100 and many have sent gifts, balloons, etc. Last night after she was asleep, Mary and Ed Davis came over and decorated the kitchen and den with a table of birthday settings, beautiful centerpiece, "happy birthday" banner, and banner from Phil and Barbara, "Happy birthday gracious lady," streamers and presents. She was astounded when she walked into the kitchen this morning. "How did this happen?" "Who did this?" "Bill, did you know about this?" We then told her of the whole plot. She was astounded and pleased. She even asked for Mary and Ed to come by so she could thank them for what they did. Around fifteen or twenty people came by the front door and left cards or gifts. And three different classes at Greater Atlanta Christian Schools sent large envelopes of letters from everyone in the class. She is exhausted emotionally now and wants to see no one for awhile, but a good night's sleep will hopefully follow. Thank you so very much for all you did to make today special for Laura.

God continues to be good to us. Laura has a very healthy anticipation of heaven and views death as a transition into the better life. I just pray that she will keep this peace that she feels now and that God will be glorified in all that happens. If he chooses to perform a miracle and heal her he certainly will be glorified. If he chooses to take her, he will be glorified by her obvious faith, hope, and peace of mind. Thank all of you for your prayers and support.

November 29, 1998

It has been over a week since I updated you on Laura's status. She continues to weaken each day. She is down to seventy-eight pounds. Laura continues to be a pillar of great faith. She is completely ready to go. She wants to hear more and more of what heaven and after death is going to be like. She has developed a very wholesome view of dying and sees it as a birth into the new life which is far greater, but she can't get a real feel for what it is going to be like. Please continue to pray for her comfort and for a peaceful passing whenever God gets ready for that to happen.

December 7, 1998

Until three days ago, Laura was coasting along on an even keel, eating and holding her weight at about seventy-eight. The nurse came today and said all vital signs were still okay, but she can tell she is much weaker. We just want her to be able to "finish the course" without a great deal of pain and suffering. Hopefully, God will be merciful and take her in an easy manner. Please pray for that as well as a pain-free existence for her last days, as much as possible. Thank you so much for your prayers, cards, and support in so many ways. God has been very good to us. Laura has a wonderful spirit and sees death as a birth into a new and wonderful life. We have been reading a lot to her about heaven and what it will be like. This is a blessing from God that her faith is so strong and that her hope is so real. At this stage of the game, the gracious sacrifice of Jesus comes to mean more than it ever has also. Anyway, thank you for your support.

December 14, 1998

Laura continues to get weaker each day. She is much weaker today. Please pray for God to be merciful to her and take her in peace and protect her against the agony and pain. God is good, even when things aren't. He will continue to be there to give us strength and he will take her and keep her safely, and she already knows that will be a great day. I'm kind of rambling, so thanks for your support and prayers.

December 23, 1998
    She is gone!
    Laura passed about 12:30 a.m. She went peacefully, but with a lot of unrest last evening. I was awake, holding her hand until about midnight, then dozed off until a little after 12:30 and found her to be very peaceful and still. She had a smile on her face when I turned over to check on her.

Six Months Later
    This is just a final wrap-up of six months of a lot of agony and struggle, yet a lot of growth in faith. I want to thank all of you for being so considerate of us and for the many messages of comfort and encouragement through these months. This has been very heart-warming to feel the prayers that so many have said they are praying in our behalf. I feel closer to God than I have felt in a long, long time. I have prayed that God will let me continue this warm relationship (hopefully without more agony to go with it) as I continue without Laura. We prayed from early in this illness that God would use it to his glory. While it has been hard to see through the suffering Laura experienced to glory, I believe that all of it is to his glory. I think her time of illness and her death were a testimony to the value of faith in God. I hope this has inspired others to want to get a right view of death from which will come perhaps a better view of life, both of which give one a deeper sense of faith in God. Please continue to pray for me as I make adjustments. I will continue to just trust God to do with it as he pleases for his glory. God Bless you and thank you from the bottom of my heart.

God was gracious to Bill. He continues his work for the Lord, and God gave him a kind and gracious lady called Betty to be his helpmeet. Bill graciously has consented to let me include this sweet story in this book.

Jule Miller

Hidden in the file drawer near the file containing Bill and Laura's story was a book that I had almost forgotten, *The Last Mile of the Way*, by Judy Miller. Judy and I had maintained a continuous connection through the years through letters and telephone calls. Her husband, Jule, had been in our home in the early 60s to conduct a home Bible study workshop. He was a kind, humble servant of God, and our children enjoyed visiting with him.

Jule was best known for the "Jule Miller Filmstrips," the *Visualized Bible Study* series introduced in 1956. The series has gone through many changes, and is still available today on DVD. In 1969, Jule was selected as Harding's Distinguished Alumnus, and again in 1998.

This is a portion from Judy's book telling the sweet story of the last day of Jule's life.

July 4, 2000: Jule's Independence Day
    The registered nurse came this morning. After checking Jule, she told us that she did not believe it would be long.
    All of us stayed by his bed all day. It broke my heart to see him so helpless and dying. I wanted to take him in my arms, hold him close to my heart . . . shelter him from death. I wanted to keep him with me, take care of him . . . never let him go. The entire family sang to him all day.
    His temperature would shoot up . . . then he would turn icy cold. His feet and his hands were like ice. I

tried to warm his hands with mine. We left his feet uncovered. That was his preference.

Ann, the hospice nurse, said, "He is a special man and deserves special care." She and Ellen took care of him all day, giving frequent doses of morphine.

All of us continued singing, praying, and talking to Jule as if he could hear us. I believe he could. I asked him to blink his eyes if he was in pain. He blinked his eyes and once again, reached out his hand for mine. I grasped it eagerly and warmly.

About 5:30 in the afternoon, Jule began to grow short of breath. He then began gasping for breath. Everyone present gathered around his bed, weeping, singing softly and sweetly, songs about heaven.

I lay as close as I could, assuring him that it was all right to let go. Now was his hour to be set free . . . for his spirit to "fly away" to our heavenly Father. "Run to Jesus," I told my beloved.

I whispered words of love . . . the joy of being his wife . . . words of gratitude for all the ways he had blessed me . . . all the ways he took such good care of me . . . for his unselfish devotion and love to me.

I asked him to tell Jesus how much we love Him and thank Him for dying for our sins. I told him, "Soon the Lord will be saying to you, "Well done, good and faithful servant. Enter into the joys of your Lord."

I stepped back a little so the children and grandchildren could tell their Daddy and Grandpa goodbye.

"Yes, Dad, I love you, Dad, Bye Grandpa. I love you."

Precious moments given by God our Father.

Three little grandsons, Jared, Joseph and Stephen, sat at the back of their Grandpa's bed, just as natural as could be.

Jule's breathing began to be quieter . . . less labored and shallower. As I gazed with tear-stained eyes into his, a miracle happened!

Jule opened his eyes and looked straight into mine. He did! He moved his lips also, as if to say, "I love you."

I gasped and so did our children. "He's looking at Mom!" someone whispered. An awesome, blessed moment.

My precious husband closed his eyes, took his last breath, and went to sleep in Jesus.

"Blessed are the saints who die in the Lord."

Immediately, the coloring in his face changed—quite strikingly. In that moment, I knew—really knew—that his spirit had gone to be with the Lord.

The body lying before us now no longer contained his spirit . . . gone, gone now, to the heavenly realms above. He will live with God forever.

The body I have loved . . . his dear face and form, lay before us . . . his wife, his children and grandchildren . . . we all adored that face and form.

Therefore, we all wept for a long time. Husbands and wives held each other and their children, while we cried our eyes out.

I was comforted during these first heart-breaking moments by Susan, my baby. She came, and placing her head on my shoulder, she cried out her pain and sorrow. I reached and took her on my lap, and held her for the longest time.

At the same time, my other five precious daughters came near to be held. We held each other . . . wept . . . then my wonderful sons came to hold and be comforted as well. My cherished daughters-in-law and sons-in-law came as well. We all held one another. God held us all.

We moved with one accord to stand around our loved one. Softly and gently, we began singing, "We Are Standing On Holy Ground."

We expressed feelings, shared memories and comforted one another. All of us were so thankful his passing had been so peaceful and without pain. How precious that all of us could be with our loved one as he passed into God's presence.

Jule looked forward to heaven. Now he is at Home— no more tears, suffering, pain or worries—ever again. His spirit is alive in the presence of our heavenly Father forever.

I told the children that I rejoiced and praised God for almost 53 years of marriage to their father. They asked me to write a book about their Dad.

In my heart I prayed, "Thank You Lord, Jule is resting in Your arms at last. "Safe in the arms of Jesus . . . sweetly his soul shall rest."

Suddenly, we all realized it was the fourth of July—a day of freedom and independence for our loved one. Jule is free—Home at last!

The medical examiner and funeral attendants arrived to carry Jule's body out of this house forever but never out of our hearts. I felt numb through and through . . . the saddest moments I have ever experienced.

The children surrounded me with loving care. I don't remember anything after that. I don't remember eating anything, taking a bath or going to bed. I do remember Susan coming to sleep with me. We held each other, praying for strength to get through this night to face a future without our beloved husband and Dad.

Claudette Jones

Dr. Jerry Jones is a well-traveled and much-sought-after teacher of God's Word. He has two master's degrees and a Th.D. from New Orleans Baptist Theological Seminary. He has taught at the undergraduate and graduate level. After the tragic death of his wife of thirty-five years, he met and married Lynn Thompson. Together they minister to hurting people who have felt the torrents of life's worst storms.

In his book *Beyond the Storm* (Howard Publishing, 1997), Dr. Jones reflects on death and loss and moving on. He has consented that I reproduce the following excerpts.

The death of my precious life-mate, Claudette DuBois Jones, was the inspiration for this book. The struggles I faced, the strength the Lord provided, the blessings of family and friends, the hope for a continued life, the courage to go on—this is what I share with you in my story.

. . . . .

Claudette taught me much about living but even more about dying.

When Claudette and I married in December 1959, I never dreamed she would precede me in death. She began her five-year battle with cancer in November 1989 and died in November 1994.

Claudette's illness began with simple back pain. After many visits to the doctor, cancer was discovered in her spinal column between her shoulder blades. During the next five years, she received radiation and chemo treatments. While she had brief periods of remission, the cancer always resurfaced in other areas of her body, and it was always inoperable.

On October 3, 1992, Claudette's birthday, the doctors told her she wouldn't live to see her next birthday. Claudette wrote an inspiring article titled "My Last Birthday," which appeared in the *Christian Woman* magazine. Claudette did live to see her birthday in 1993 and in 1994, but because of her gradual decline, she eventually required supplemental oxygen, a wheelchair, and constant care.

When Claudette realized that the treatments were only buying her time and were never going to cure her, she began to prepare herself, me, and the rest of the family for her death. She kept a journal of her thoughts. She boxed up items she wanted each child to have. She made last visits to friends, relatives, and her mother. She discussed her funeral plans in detail with me and told me what to do with the family the first Christmas without her.

In spite of pain and the pressures of her illness, Claudette maintained a positive and cheerful attitude. She had few periods of depression. In fact, those who visited her left feeling blessed by her. Claudette had the ability to see humor in serious situations. Two situations I will always remember. One of the side effects of the morphine she was taking for pain was uncontrollable jerking—she would drop books or pencils or even slap herself accidentally. On a routine visit, a nurse asked, "Claudette, how are you doing with 'the jerks'?"

Claudette said, "I'm doing just fine; I've gotten used to them."

"How did you get used to 'the jerks'?" the nurse asked!

The second situation occurred in connection with her medication. One morning she sat down near me in the family room and asked me to dial a number on the telephone as she picked up the receiver. I didn't know who I was dialing, but after a minute I realized that she was talking to the Wal-Mart pharmacy. She told the pharmacist that she needed to have a prescription refilled and noted that the prescription was for a sixty-day supply, and then she said, "I am a terminal cancer patient; so I only need a thirty-day supply." When she hung up the phone, I was at a loss for words. How should I respond? I finally said, "I imagine you wouldn't buy green bananas, either!"

The last week of Claudette's life was difficult. Because she chose to die at home, we had to rent a hospital bed for her. She objected to the bed because she saw it as a step down in her recovery, even though she knew she was dying. Two of my three children, as well as several close friends, were present when she died. When death and relief finally came for her, the atmosphere in the house was joyful; we all knew that Claudette was now free from pain and that she had won the victory.

Seeing one you love slowly die over a period of five years isn't easy. I know. Losing a loved one in an accidental death is hard, and losing a loved one due to unexpected health problems is likewise difficult. Each type of death carries with it a different set of emotions. Recovering from the death of a loved one is a very individual matter. There is no right way or wrong way to handle death and grief. Even though no two situations are ever the same, I believe that the following lessons I learned along my journey can bless the lives of others.

View death as a reality for all people. Despite the precautions we take, we can't control how death will come. Death brings pain; pain is the price we pay for love. If you didn't love so deeply, the pain of loss wouldn't be so great. Expressing grief is natural. Paul declared that he would have had "sorrow upon sorrow" had Epaphroditus died (Phil. 2:27)

Bring closure to the death of your loved one. In my case, I had the assurance that I had done everything I could to sustain Claudette's life and make it comfortable. We had time to reaffirm our love and appreciation for one another. Once she was gone, I needed to close that chapter of my life. However, some don't have the opportunity to say and do all they can for the deceased, and this can result in guilt. The one left behind to grieve must accept the fact that no situation is ever handled perfectly and that doing it differently might not have been better than the way it was done. There's nothing more you can do for the loved one who died; you must go on with your life.

Learn to deal with the newfound freedom one day at a time. Have these relationships in place before and after the death of a spouse. You need some sounding boards for your thoughts and feeling. Choose those who will be open and honest with you and who may, at times, disagree with you.

Do something for yourself. If you have been a caregiver for a long time, you need to invest in yourself a little. I'm not suggesting that you buy a new red sports car, but a shopping spree might be in order, as well as some short trips with friends.

Translate your loved one from the present to memories. Accept the reality that your loved one isn't coming back. You will always have memories to cherish, but you will never have his or her physical presence again. Death isn't the extinguishing of a light; rather, it is the turning off of a lamp because the dawn has come.

Learn to live life among problems. Sometimes problems are a result of our actions, but many times, they come through no fault of our own. Life has never been problem free. You may declare the unfairness of life, but this too is a reality of living.

You can be a better person as a result of living through adversity. When others face the same challenges you have faced, you can speak with credibility. You have a deeper empathy for others. Your ability to minister to others will be enhanced.

Trust in the Lord's wisdom—anyway. Adversity demands a trust in God previously unknown. The answer to *Why?* can be forever unanswered. Failure to see good in adversity is common, especially when there is no rhyme or reason for it, but you must trust anyway. It isn't easy to walk by faith and not by sight.

Creating a new agenda for your life isn't wrong. There can be more than one plan for your life, and finding a new direction can be exciting and challenging. Choose to bloom where you have been planted. The roads of bitterness and self-pity bring unhappiness and depression. You may feel limited in your ability to go on with life, but going on will ultimately bring the greatest sense of accomplishment and happiness.

Timothy Hill

Jerry Hill, the founder of Timothy Hill Children's Ranch, was initially a preacher in Riverhead, New York, throughout the 60s and 70s. He and his wife Fern opened their home and hearts to dozens of foster children who were homeless and in need of temporary housing. Their older son Timothy saw the painful hardships and emotional suffering that the children had endured, and he was deeply affected. He told his parents he wanted someday to "build a place where homeless kids could live, be loved, feel safe and have wide open spaces to ride horses."

Timothy began working at age twelve to save money for the land where his dream could become a reality. He worked three paper routes and had already begun contacting real estate agents in search of property. His mother, Fern, recalls fielding several return calls from disgruntled real estate agents. She simply explained to them that she could not discourage her son from following his dream.

On May 11, 1972, a bicycle-truck accident ended Timothy's life at the age of thirteen. His mother, wanting a way to commemorate his life, wrote a book entitled *Graduation to Glory* (Star Bible Publications, 1974). The book recounts Timothy's altruistic years and his visionary dream of opening up a ranch for homeless children. Friends and neighbors responded spontaneously by creating a memorial fund earmarked "for Timothy's ranch." Jerry and Fern adopted their son's dream, and God has blessed the journey ever since. Timothy Hill Children's Ranch opened its doors in Riverhead on November 15, 1980, a seventy-acre, farm-style campus. For twenty-eight years it has been a safe haven for hundreds of children during desperate times of abuse, neglect, and crisis.

Bram and Kopeland Gallegos

While I was writing this book, our family experienced an event in 2009 that was near and dear to our hearts.

My granddaughter, Amanda, and her husband, Joseph, are the proud parents of a two-year-old son,

Ethan. He brought so much joy into their lives that they earnestly desired more children. So they prayed together and separately that if it was God's will Amanda would be able to conceive again, even though she had experienced difficulty in her first pregnancy. This is the story that she told me.

Amanda got pregnant quickly, and she and Joseph basked in the excitement and joy of having another baby on the way. Soon, however, Amanda developed severe complications. When she went to her doctor for her six weeks check-up, he insisted on performing a sonogram immediately.

The doctor announced the somber results.

"You are going to have identical twins," he said. "They are conjoined. I advise you to terminate the pregnancy immediately."

Amanda stood up, put both her hands on her hips, and angrily shouted, "I will not!"

Amanda returned home and told Joseph the entire story. They immediately prayed together, "God, be with us as we go through this difficult trial. We seek your will in our lives."

Although Amanda was greatly troubled by the disturbing news, she was able to sleep that night. But in the middle of the night she awoke abruptly. She felt that God had caused her to wake up. She looked at the clock. It was five. She softly got out of bed and tiptoed into the living room. The entire house was quiet. Joseph and Ethan were both asleep. Amanda sat in the living room and started talking to God. She felt his presence. She asked him to quiet her anxious heart and to reveal his truth to her. A feeling of relief filled her soul and she went back to bed. During her time asleep, she had a dream. God showed her vividly two beautiful identical twin boys with red hair. They were separate and perfect in every way. She did not tell Joseph her dream next morning.

When Joseph was on his way to work that morning, a stranger—a man on the street—came up to him and said, "May God bless you with many sons." Immediately the stranger walked away.

As the man's figure disappeared in the distance, Joseph wondered why the man had spoken to him, and he pondered what this meant.

That night Joseph told Amanda this story, she told him about her dream. They both wondered and were determined not to terminate the pregnancy. Maybe God was saying the twins that Amanda was carrying were in fact normal.

Seven months later—painful months filled with complications, tears of agony, impatience, and prayers that the ordeal be over—Amanda entered the hospital in Las Cruces, New Mexico. After an examination, she was immediately airlifted to Dallas for the delivery.

The doctors explained that according to medical records the boys should not even be alive, because they had no pancreas. The twins had two heads on one body, and a sonogram did not reveal how their internal organs were functioning. The doctors were certain they would not live very long. They explained that the boys would never be off of feeding tubes.

After absorbing the news, Amanda and Joseph affirmed that they loved their little boys dearly, just as they were. They wanted to take the boys home to Las Cruces and give them all the loving care available in their short lifespan.

The doctors replied, "They will need twenty-four-hour care. This will be a very demanding ordeal. Are you both willing to accept that?"

Amanda and Joseph's immediate reply was, "Yes! We will love them! We do not want to throw away the tremendous blessing that God has given us."

Amanda's thoughts went back to the fight with the doctor all along the pregnancy to abort her little boys. "I will look every day," she thought silently, "for the blessing that God has in store for me."

Arrangements were made for Amanda, Joseph, the twins, and Amanda's mother, Diana, to fly back to Las Cruces. Bram and Kopeland were the first conjoined twins born at the Medical Center of Dallas to go home alive. Most conjoined twins die shortly after birth. Soon after they were home, the boys were each able to eat four ounces of formula.

It was difficult to figure out how to help the boys. They had two heads joined to one body. They had one and a half hearts fused together. They had two stomachs, and both boys were happy and responded with smiles when their little stomachs were full. Giving them a bath and changing their clothes was a challenge.

Sometimes the obstacles seemed overwhelming, but Amanda and Joseph worked through them prayerfully, and somehow each problem was solved.

God sent many people to help during these stressful times. Friends, family, church friends, and others prayed and brought food and gifts. Civic organizations in town held fundraisers to pay medical expenses, and later, funeral expenses. Hugs were plentiful.

Amanda said it was amazing what love could do. The boys did well, and she was amazed at the great bond she and the twins made among themselves. It was something she would not change for anything in the world. The brief life of these boys touched the lives of many others. Amanda felt honored to hold heaven in her arms and to glimpse what God's love is like. She was blessed to see that God had done something so amazing that men couldn't explain it. She knew that God had used her as a vessel to bring her boys into the world.

The twins lived exactly thirty days. The family enjoyed the awesome gift of having their boys with them during Christmas. They passed away on December 30.

Amanda held them all that day so they would not be alone. She watched them die a slow and painful death. She felt helpless when the pacifiers could not take the pain away.

She sat in the chair and cried. She cried out to God and asked him to show her that he was there and that he had heard her prayer.

When she had said amen, she looked up and saw Jesus. He was standing by the rocking chair, watching her like a proud father. He was beautiful.

Amanda turned her head and stared at him for a while. She experienced a peace so amazing and thick that she could fall sleep in it. She knew that no matter what, she was going to be all right.

Joseph came over and knelt beside her, and they watched the boys as they lay sleeping in Amanda's arms.

Amanda looked over, and Jesus was standing behind Joseph. She could feel Jesus' arms around her. She knew that he had come to take the boys home. He was waiting until they were ready.

That night the boys became worse. They turned pale and then blue as the night progressed. They screamed in agonizing pain and struggled for every breath.

Friends came.

When oxygen no longer helped, they prayed fervently and waited. Amanda couldn't bear to see the boys suffer any longer. They prayed for direction from God. They asked him if they should remove the oxygen.

God spoke to Joseph and said to him, "Why deny these little ones paradise?"

Joseph removed the oxygen and held the twins in his arms until their labored breathing completely stopped.

They were gone.

It was the most difficult decision they had ever had to make.

After the boys were gone, Amanda was overwhelmed by an indescribably painful emptiness. After going to God's Word for answers, and after many prayers, Amanda can now say what they have learned from their ordeal.

They learned how great was God's love for them. As one parent to another, they said, "Now we can see how painful it was for God to send his Son to the cross to die. What love God has for us! We didn't understand that great pain until now. He sent his Son to die on the cross for your sins and ours. We are sure that he felt the pain that we experienced, and he knew that nothing could be done to stop it. That shows how strongly God wanted to have a loving, working relationship with us. That's an awesome love!"

God has been good to us through all of this. He has given us a peace that we had never experienced before.

As I write these words, it has now been six weeks since the boys passed away.

Amanda missed the boys so much that she started having panic attacks, some of them very frightening. She prayed and asked God to heal her from these attacks. She did not tell Joseph about her prayers, or how frightened she felt.

But God put it into Joseph's heart to get her a very special Valentine's Day gift, the very thing she needed. He gave her a silver locket from Zale's with their "Shared Hearts" design outlined in diamonds. A small heart inside a larger one.

Amanda put pictures of the boys inside. Now whenever she feels upset or frightened, she holds the necklace tight to her heart and knows that the boys are still with her. God is good!

Amanda knows that God has another set of twins for her. She saw them in her dream. She holds on to that dream and waits. She believes, just as Sarah and Abraham did, that in time God will give her twins to love, for nothing is impossible with God. She is thankful that he let her be a part of the miracle of Bram and Kopeland and allowed her to hold a piece of heaven for thirty days. God is good!

Amanda said that Grandpa always told her, "The weak give up and the strong almost do."

She prays that God will keep her strong.

Chapter 8
A White Stone

He who has an ear, let him hear what the Spirit
says to the churches. To him who overcomes, I
will give some of the hidden manna to eat. And I
will give him a white stone, and on the stone a
new name written which no one knows except
him who receives it.
> —Revelation 2:17 (NKJV)

God lit a flame and kindled a fire deep in my soul
by putting two scenes in my heart that would not
leave me. The first was placed there by our great-
grandson, Nathan.

Weeks after the funeral, Nathan looked at me with
deep, searching eyes.

"Mamaw," he asked, "where is Papaw?"

I looked into his deeply probing eyes still peering
at me.

"He's in Heaven," I said slowly.

"Where is Heaven, Mamaw?"

I tried to answer, but tears blurred my eyes and
my words stuck in my throat, and I could not
answer.

After Nathan had gone home, his question kept
stirring the ashes of a spark in my heart. What was
wrong with me? I didn't know how to answer him!

Later that day my eyes fell on a small white quartz
stone that Harold always kept on his office desk. He

had carefully written on it, in bold, black ink, "Revelation 2:17."

"God," I prayed, "you know that I have heard Harold preach over and over again about the white stone. Why could I not answer our little four-year-old great-grandson?"

Two years passed. Then the second scene was placed in my heart, again when Nathan and Diana came to visit. I watched them as they put a new puzzle together. Nathan became frustrated when he couldn't find any pieces that matched. Diana patiently showed him the secret. First, find all the pieces with a straight line and put them together to form a frame. After that, the rest of the pieces will fit together in the right place.

After they went home, I pondered over that concept, and my mind drifted back to the late 1970s. I had not graduated from Terre Haute Commercial College—in spite of what I had written to Harold's commanding officer!—so twenty-five years later I returned to college to complete a degree in accounting.

My first class was a computer systems management course. I dived right into the material and spent hours digesting the details. When I walked into class to take the mid-term exam, I felt confident and fully expected to make one of the highest scores in the class. I was one of the first to complete the exam, and I could not wait to see what the results would be.

In a few days I returned to class, and to my complete amazement, I saw red check marks covering all of the pages! I saw a big, bold D-minus at the top of the front page. I had just barely passed. In a state of complete shock, I rushed home and called our daughter Cathy, who was a senior in college in another state. Since Cathy always made extremely good grades, I thought she could help me. I must pass that course! It was required for my accounting degree, and my current job depended on my completing these courses.

Cathy laughed and told me to calm down. She told me the best course of action was to make an appointment with the professor. She was sure he would be happy to help me.

The next day I made the appointment. The professor listened intently as I explained how many hours I had spent studying and pouring over the material. I had never missed a single class. I couldn't believe my low score.

He was kind and patient and looked over my wrong answers. In a matter of seconds he told me that they all fell into a definite pattern. I was spending too much time on the details, and I had not learned the broad, overall concepts he was trying to teach.

I thanked him, and as I was leaving his office, I noticed a large sign nailed to his door: "A mind expanded will never return to its original size."

At the end of the course I passed the final exam and made an A-minus in the course.

I wrote about this experience in my journal and wondered whether I had studied the Bible in the same way. Did I pour over all of the details with an attitude that I had all of the right answers? Had I been reading the Bible to prove how right I was and to focus on the faults of others?

That question in my journal of long ago lingered in my mind. So did Nathan's question. And of course there was Harold's ever-present stone! So I decided it was time to study the matter further.

Petrified Stones

In Harold's office I discovered a well-worn copy of William Barclay's *New Testament Words* (Philadelphia: Westminster Press, 1964). Harold had used it frequently in his studies.

One of the chapters explained the words *pôroun*, "to harden," and *pôrôsis*, "a hardening." Together these words occur eight times in the New Testament, and they have in back of them the word *pôros*, a stone similar to marble. Jesus had used this kind of stone as an image of the heart that had hardened and become as impenetrable as marble.

"Hardening" is the mental condition of a person who cannot see the lesson that the events are designed to teach him. The words convey three variations of meaning: loss of feeling, blindness, and inability to see. When any of these conditions occur, we simply cannot comprehend the lessons that God intends for us to see. Our minds become so controlled by our own pre-set ideas and perceptions of reality that we cannot see the providential working of God. Our eyes and ears have filters because of our past experiences and we refuse to allow new ideas to penetrate our thoughts. Barclay wrote, "If a man erects his ideas into supreme authority for long enough he will in the end be incapable of receiving the ideas of God" (p. 239).

This lesson hit me very hard during the writing of this book. Our daughter Janice had reviewed a draft of the chapter about Harold's funeral and asked me to put in more details. In fact, I had almost completely ignored that entire scene. So after much prayer, on a cold, snowy, wintry day, I tried one more time to view the DVD of the service. I was amazed that I was able to view it as many times as I needed to transcribe it for this book. Then I read the new chapter and reflected on each scene. I realized how blind I had been to the reality of what had happened, not only during the funeral but even up to that day. I had been blind!

The Potter and the Clay

> Yet you, Lord, are our Father. We are the clay, you are the potter; we are all the work of your hand.
> —Isaiah 64:8

> But the pot he was shaping from the clay was marred in his hands; so the potter formed it into another pot, shaping it as seemed best to him.
> —Jeremiah 18:4

As I thumbed further through Barclay's *New Testament Words*, I found a well-worn page that

Harold had marked and notated extensively, on the Greek word *kalos*. Harold had marked this passage:

In Genesis 1:8 God looked at the world which he had made, he saw that it was good (*kalos*). The name of Christ is said to be *kalos* as the beauty of holiness. *Kalos* stressed the fact that the best advocate of Christianity to the outsider is the sheer attractive loveliness of the life of the true Christian. The New Testament teaches that the best missionary weapon is a great example—a person who lets the mind of Christ flow through him or her to everyone whom they meet (p. 157).

After I read that, I put the book down and thought about the people in my saints file. I took a deep breath and realized how God had allowed me to know so many people who were outstanding examples, and had allowed me to read about my courageous ancestor Asa Frakes. Did this mean that God had placed a great responsibility on me to pick up the blood-stained banner of Christ and share it with others?

I remembered a challenge that God had given me. I was deeply concerned about the actions of someone whom I loved dearly—actions that I knew would lead to disaster. After many agonizing prayers for that person, I went to the Bible and studied this passage:

The Lord's bond-servant must not be quarrelsome, but be kind to all, able to teach, patient when wronged, with gentleness correcting those who are in opposition, if perhaps God may grant them repentance leading to the knowledge of the truth, and they may come to their senses and escape from the snare of the devil, having been held captive by him to do his will (2 Tim. 2:24–26 NASB).

I copied the passage out and inserted the name of the person I was concerned about. I read it aloud during my daily prayer time and asked God to grant this person repentance. Weeks dragged into months, when a great transformation took place! I cried tears of joy and remembered:

> Those who sow with tears will reap with songs of joy. Those who go out weeping, carrying seed to sow, will return with songs of joy, carrying sheaves with them (Ps. 126:5–6).

The Stone at the Tomb

My study of stones led me next to a sermon Harold had preached many times, "The Faith to See Angels." The story concerned the death, burial, and resurrection of Jesus Christ, and it was taken from the following passage in the Gospel of Matthew.

> After the Sabbath, at dawn on the first day of the week, Mary Magdalene and the other Mary went to look at the tomb.
> There was a violent earthquake, for an angel of the Lord came down from heaven and, going to the tomb, rolled back the stone and sat on it. His appearance was like lightning, and his clothes were white as snow. The guards were so afraid of him that they shook and became like dead men.
> The angel said to the women, "Do not be afraid, for I know that you are looking for Jesus, who was crucified. He is not here; he has risen, just as he said. Come and see the place where he lay. Then go quickly and tell his disciples: 'He has risen from the dead and is going ahead of you into Galilee. There you will see him.' Now I have told you."
> So the women hurried away from the tomb, afraid yet filled with joy, and ran to tell his disciples.

Suddenly Jesus met them. "Greetings," he said. They came to him, clasped his feet and worshiped him. Then Jesus said to them, "Do not be afraid. Go and tell my brothers to go to Galilee; there they will see me." (Matt. 28:1–10)

The Memorial Stone

Harold always pointed out the dedication of the women to walk alone to the cemetery while it was still dark, since in their culture superstition was rampant.

They also had faith to believe that God would roll away the heavy stone at the door of the tomb so they could anoint Jesus' body with spices. God rewarded their faith. An angel of the Lord rolled back the stone and talked to them telling them of the risen Christ. Mary Magdalene was rewarded by talking to the two angels in white and talking to the risen Christ.

The Living Stone

We are going down the valley one by one, and we are the living stones—not the church, but we as individuals. Collectively we individuals make up the great body of the church.

The Memorial Stone (Joshua 3–4)

God challenged Joshua with the mission of getting a group of Israelites across the Jordan River so they could claim the Land of Promise. Three times God encouraged Joshua by telling him to remember his promises in the past to Moses and others. So Joshua obeyed God.

When all of the people had completely crossed over the Jordan, God told Joshua to make memorial stones to remind their children and grandchildren of the great acts of God that they had witnessed that day.

So Joshua set up twelve stones in the middle of the Jordan River. These represented each of the twelve tribes. The people were instructed to constantly remind their children of the deliverance that God provided because they had trusted him and obeyed him, even when they were afraid.

Our Family Memorial

On June 29, 1988, Harold penned these words for a bulletin article.

It is so important that fathers and mothers provide their children with little memorials. As I write this I am sitting at an old round oak table. This was where the family ate, talked about the events of the day, dreamed sometimes, talked about God, prayed a great deal, and discussed our problems. Awhile ago my married daughter and I sat around this table discussing a problem. Her thoughts and ideas flowed smoothly. This old table reminded her that she had roots, and was a part. Most of all it was here that we had met God many times, and discussed his deliverance in answer to our prayers.

Once when I was in Belgium an elderly friend took me to the "Plains of Waterloo." He pointed out to me in great detail the battle array, and how each opposing force conducted the battle. Though my friend was generations removed from that great conflict, yet I could see in his eyes and in his voice that he was a part of that scene. He was a Frenchman, and this was his country. He showed me great cathedrals dating back to the twelfth century, and for the first time in my life I envied my friend. His roots were deep and strong. Our nation is a young nation and our memorials, monuments, and shrines are young, because they commemorate people and events just yesterday. But how important memorials are as we try to write our own book of antiquities so that all generations can see, feel, and be part of something with roots and substance!

God understands that man constantly needs to be reminded. How quickly sometimes we forget. One of the beautiful attributes of the ancients is the handing down, from one generation to the next, of the working of God among his people. How wide-eyed those children must have been as they listened to the elders tell in great detail how God delivered Israel that day. These same children someday would tell the grand story to their children, and so add another page to the book of antiquity.

Give your children a round oak table.

Now the white quartz stones that Harold placed on all of the pulpits and on his personal desk made sense to me. They were his way of reminding us of our priceless reward of being able to personally see Jesus the Christ face to face and to receive our unique reward.

The Master's Hand

In the late 1970s Harold gave a television devotion and told the following story.

Many years ago, a woman was talking with the artist John Ruskin, and she mentioned that a favorite handkerchief of hers had been ruined by a spot of ink. Ruskin was moved by the loss, because he saw that the handkerchief meant a great deal to her. He asked if he might have her handkerchief. The woman agreed, but wondered why he would want such a worthless piece of material.

Several days later, Ruskin brought the handkerchief back and presented it to the woman. Starting from the spot on the handkerchief, he had drawn a beautiful, intricate pattern. When he gave the handkerchief back to her now, it was indeed beautiful.

Many times the things we think ugly become beautiful in the hands of the Master. "It is good for me that I have been afflicted; that I might learn thy statutes" (Ps. 119:71 KJV).

Robert Leighton, the great preacher, once remarked after a period of illness that he had learned more about God from his bed than he had learned previously in all of his life. So it is possible that in the hands of God, something that is seemingly ugly and worthless becomes beautiful and of great value. The Apostle Paul had a thorn in his flesh, and yet out of that weakness he was taught grace, mercy, gentleness, and kindness.

God does the same thing with us day by day. He takes our lives, which to us sometimes seem worthless, and he makes something valuable. He takes something which on the outside may seem ugly, and yet he works with it and makes something beautiful. This is to his glory.

God never works with beautiful vessels. There is no glory in that. He never takes something strong, because there is no glory there. He takes the weak. He takes the imperfect. And in his hand, and with his loving care, he makes something beautiful and strong.

Rocky Marciano, one time heavyweight boxing champion, was a man noted for his endless style of oppressing his opponent. He could fight steadily for fifteen rounds. Most people do not realize that when Marciano first started, he had no stamina. So he spent hours upon hours in a swimming pool punching in water, and out of that weakness grew his fantastic stamina—his ability to press on.

This is how God works with us. This is how we grow. "All things work together for good to those who love God, to those who are called according to His purpose" (Rom. 8:28 NKJV). You are not worthless in the hands of God. The Master's hand will make you valuable and beautiful.

What the White Stone Means to Me

As I think back through the years, and as I reflect on the volumes of commentaries that I have studied about the white stone, here is what the white stone means to me.

It is a memorial and a reminder. I have one of Harold's white quartz stones with Revelation 2:17 in my bedroom next to my clock. I see it the first thing every morning. It quietly reminds and calls me each morning to my special time with God. As I read the Bible and hear God's voice, as I pray and tell God what is on my heart, as I write in my prayer journal and put all my hurts, fears, and anxieties on the written page, it cleans and clears my mind for a bright new day.

I am beginning to wonder if the precious, unique, white stone that God will give me—one that only God and I will know—will allow me to see myself as God sees me. It will show me the many times that God and Christ pulled me up from the quicksand of my flawed thinking, the dark moments of my life, my wavering, weary, worried, wounded spirit, my unforgiving and unthankful heart, my unkind words and selfish pride. Then the endless list turns into sweet whispers of divine love for a worthless soul such as I.

Chapter 9

Beholding the Face of God

I did not see a temple in the city, because the Lord God Almighty and the Lamb are its temple. The city does not need the sun or the moon to shine on it, for the glory of God gives it light, and the Lamb is its lamp.

—Revelation 21:22–23

No longer will there be any curse. The throne of God and of the Lamb will be in the city, and his servants will serve him. They will see his face, and his name will be on their foreheads.

—Revelation 22:3–4

I miss Harold most in the fall, the time of year as I write these words. I am vividly reminded of the finality of his absence as the time draws closer to the time of his death, September 18—also our daughter Janice's birthday. This past year has been a time of sifting what to remember from the past and what to forget.

One of the most difficult adjustments I have had to make as a widow is sitting at the old round oak table eating alone. The food I prepare for myself never tastes good or satisfying. I remember the many meals that Harold and I prepared over the years for family and friends. Harold always enjoyed his meals and spent much time making dishes like Greek moussaka, German sauerbraten, homemade noodles for an Italian feast, and all the various dishes for a Mexican treat. In our many travels and in the diversified cultures where we have lived, Harold always picked out their favorite dishes. One time his love for homemade ice cream led him to find recipes for dozens of flavors, to make gallons of every flavor, and to share them at gatherings of family and friends.

I remember Harold's last words before he fell into the coma that lasted until his death. The memory still burns in my heart how he woke Janice in the middle of the night, how we all gathered around him and gave him permission to leave and go on, how his face changed and he said, "God's House! Beautiful! Let's Go!" Debbie believes that his final words mirror how God blessed him: Harold loved to build houses, and God validated that love by showing him his own house—and of course it was beautiful.

I remember Harold's unquenchable thirst for the mind of God, expressed in the words of the Bible. In our quiet times we would read, talk, ponder, and pray about things we didn't understand. His preaching contained sermon series with such titles as "The Beatitudes—Why God Made Man," "The Disciple Jesus Loved—The Writings of the Apostle John," "The Miracles of Jesus Christ," "The Parables of Jesus Christ," and "Bible Character Studies." He encouraged the churches we were with to read through the entire Bible in a year. Then each Sunday he would preach a sermon from the portion of Scripture that we had read during the previous week. The project started out as a great help for the churches, but it ended up as a great encouragement for us to continue keeping on when we faced challenges.

Dead men speak, and their works follow them— either good or evil. I am thankful that I made cassette tapes of all of Harold's lessons and sermons and preserved them. As a memorial to him, I have had the tapes rerecorded in digital format for our children and grandchildren. Harold preached many times about the Logos of God and how he believed that a word spoken never dies.

I remember Harold's constant prayer, in public and private, that God would quickly take him home after his work was done. He believed strongly in a loving God that he called Abba Father, or sometimes Daddy—a God who loves us and has a divine purpose for us. It is up to us to pick up the banner of this divine purpose and act on it. If we do, we will live the best possible life that can be lived. Harold always thanked God for the opportunity to serve him by proclaiming his word and building churches. I realize now that I lived in the shadow of a great servant of God who loved God even more than he loved me. That was what made him such a loving husband.

I look back with tears of joy to our fiftieth wedding anniversary, about which I have already told a little in a previous chapter. For me the crowning joy of the event was a song that Harold sang especially for me. He had originally sung it to me before we married. We had dated for a year, and he walked over early one Saturday morning in the spring and sang the

song to wake me up. I think he had composed it
himself.

> I come to your window
> In the cool of the morn,
> To sing very softly
> As a new day is born.
>
> I sing very softly
> So no one can hear.
> I love you, my darling.
> I love, you my dear.
>
> The roads ever beckon
> As a new day appears.
> Come out, my darling,
> Before anyone hears.
>
> I sing very softly
> So no one can hear.
> I love you, my darling.
> I love you, my dear.

I remember Harold teaching that God has no
grandchildren, and I am coming to understand this
more and more. We are either children of God or
none of His. Each of us must seek and find a
relationship with God on our own. We are not judged
as a church or a family, but as individuals who make
our own choices and live out the consequences. I
miss Harold terribly, but I know I depended too
heavily on him for my own spiritual maturity. I
needed to grow more on my own. I am beginning to
sense the wisdom in that.

I remember a summer evening in California in the
1960s, when our five children were teenagers. We

were sitting around our oak table after dinner, discussing the events of the day. I cleared the dishes away and served our favorite dessert: Harold's homemade ice cream.

When the ice cream bowls were empty, Harold looked around the table, cleared his throat, and said, "Children, we need to have a serious discussion. I just learned that some of you are doing things that will harm you severely."

"Dad, what are you talking about?"

"Who told you?"

"Who did it?"'

"I want to tell you a story," Harold said, and paused.

"It was August 1938 in southern Indiana. I was eight years old. About three miles from our home was an old pond. The coal mine took its water from this pond to operate its boilers. I was taught at a very early age not to go to this pond because it was crawling with snakes. Periodically my dad and the other men would take their guns and dynamite and go down to this old pond to try to get rid of as many snakes as possible. But I also knew that around the banks of this old pond were the most beautiful cattails to be found within miles.

"One day I decided that I wanted some cattails. I knew that my dad had told me not to go. I had been to the pond with the men when they were killing snakes. But I said to myself, 'I'm old enough, and if I take the necessary precautions, nothing is going to happen.' So I went to the bank of that old pond. I got a good-sized club, rolled up my pants legs, and slowly walked in. I thrashed the water with that club. I was doing great. I'd go along and cut cattails, and before long I had a whole armload.

"The first thing I noticed, however, was that my club was in the way. I really didn't think now there was any need to exercise any caution. So I threw my old club away and went ahead cutting cattails. As I continued cutting, all of a sudden I felt a great pain in the calf of my left leg. I raised my leg up and there was a big old water moccasin hanging on my leg! I knew enough about snakes not to run home. Even now after all these years, I can still remember vividly an eight-year-old boy struggling *not* to run home, but to walk very slowly and to remain calm. By the time I reached home, I was quite ill. I was feverish. The snake's venom had already done its work.

"I remember the days and nights that followed this incident. I can still recall the room where I rolled and tossed in pain, and I can still see my bed. Many times I have looked back through the years and remembered that scene. I have asked myself many times the question, 'Why?' After many years I realized that this incident in my life was a blessing— a divine blessing. I have been able to look back and ask why and understand then, why you and I sometimes do the things that we do in life.

"Each of us knows that sin is a terrible thing. It separates us from our God. It damns our eternal soul. Once we have been bitten by that serpent, it can be fatal. Why then armed with all of this knowledge, do you and I continually, habitually, seek after those things that we should not seek after and do? As I look back to that August day, I thought what I really wanted was cattails. Now I know what I really wanted was to say to my dad and to all of those men who had warned me, 'You don't know what you are talking about.' I wanted to say to them, 'I am the exception. I can take my club. I can arm myself with precautions and I can engage in this sin and nothing is going to happen to me.'

"When Dad saw me coming home, he gave me an affectionate hug and quickly called the doctor. He did not punish me. Later he said he knew that I had learned my lesson, and that I would now respect snakes."

"Why did you tell us that story, Dad?"

"I just wanted you to know that I still love you. You are all unique snowflakes. You are all very special in your own way.

"That's how God feels about us. He loves us just like we are. He knows that we are weak and need help. He is always ready to forgive if we ask him. God knows that if we reject him and go ahead and sin, we will suffer painful consequences. However, if we decide to change directions and ask for God's help, he will always give us the direction and strength to walk through our struggles to overcome our unwise choices.

"So just like my painful snake bite, sin has painful consequences. But as God heals us when we come to him, we learn to respect the goodness of God and the wisdom in his word, the Bible."

One by one the children got up from the table, gave their Dad a hug and silently walked away.

We are being slowly resurrected now as we daily face Jesus the Christ by receiving his word, his *logos*, into our lives. Then at that day it will be no surprise when we are given the gift of seeing him face to face clearly and not with blurred vision as before.

After months of prayerful work writing this book, I became impatient to complete it—to write this last chapter. Then something happened that slowed me down.

I was walking toward the entrance of church on a Sunday Morning near the end of March, speaking to a visitor, when I stepped up onto the curb, lost my balance, and fell. I was stunned. I had fallen on my right side and could not move!

Immediately I was surrounded by a host of people trying to figure out how to help me. The look of concern on their faces terrified me. What had happened to me? What was I going to do now?

Before I could contemplate the answers, someone rolled over a wheelchair to transport me to the church office. Soon I was surrounded by three compassionate nurses. They put my arm in a temporary sling and put ice on my elbow. They took my blood pressure and examined me for other wounds. They washed my bloody face and examined my jaw and the side of my head that had hit the concrete. Someone found my daughter Diana, who was already seated in the sanctuary, and brought her to the office. She whisked me away to the emergency room. There it was determined that I had broken my right elbow and my big toe and severely injured my face.

Immediately—from one footstep to the next—my world had changed!

Harold had always said that when you pray for specific needs, fasten your seat belt, because God will answer your request—although not necessarily in the way you expected, so you will know the answer came from God.

Very soon I discovered that my entire mindset changed. I was dependent on others to help me. I discovered that accepting help was more painful than my injuries. Before falling I had had no idea that my stubborn pride was such a problem!

God taught me many valuable lessons as friends took me to church, the doctor, the grocery store, the post office, the bank, as they cleaned my house and prepared my meals. I work one day a week at an accounting office, and the owners, Jim and Randy, picked me up for work and took me home. Our son, John, told me that I should not rob these people of the joy that God gives them from serving.

I wondered if God felt the same way about our accepting the grace that he has provided for us through his Son Jesus Christ. Does our stubborn pride say, "I'll do it myself!" Do we say, in effect, "I'll gather my own cattails, thank you!" Does this attitude get in the way of our believing and accepting God's grace? I didn't know this pride was in me before the fall.

It is worth thinking about for all of us. Do we accept the precious gift of salvation that Jesus Christ offers us? When we were his enemies he died on the cross to forgive our sins and to make us acceptable to live with God in Heaven. If we confessed that Jesus the Christ is the Son of God, that he was resurrected from the grave as prophesied in the Old Testament as the promised Messiah, if we were baptized for the remission of our sins, then the Holy Spirit from God entered our being and gave us salvation from our sins, past, present, and future. We must accept this great gift. We do not need to beg every day for this forgiveness. We must accept it as a fact and then forgive ourselves and thank God daily for this wonderful blessing and for the privilege of sharing this great news with others.

As we acknowledge the gift of the Holy Spirit in our lives, we become more aware of his presence as he teaches us how to live a new life pleasing to God. As he teaches, he convicts us of the sins that have blinded our eyes. He patiently teaches us to understand the words in the Bible that we were unable to comprehend in the past. He leads us on a straight path that will protect us from the hidden, deceitful traps that Satan has designed to distract us from our Heavenly rewards and our present peace from God.

If you don't experience this peace now, ask yourself why not? If you have been a child of God for many years and are still burdened with sleepless nights, anger, hostility, a critical spirit, fading energy, and an unforgiving nature, rethink your one-on-one relationship with God. Forgiveness is the golden key that opens up heaven's pearly gates. Accepting God's forgiveness for us is contingent on our forgiving the people in our daily life.

If your parents were Christians, or if you belong to a dynamic church, or if you are married to a strong, spiritual person, be especially wary. God wants a one-on-one relationship with you. No one can save you but Jesus Christ! It came to me as a stinging truth when I realized that I must not worship the messenger who brings God's word, but worship God alone.

In my life with Harold, it was easy for me to depend on him for my spiritual nourishment. After all, he was the preacher I had prayed to marry. But now I wonder whether I placed a burden on him that God did not want him to have.

After all, we are reminded in the Bible not to idolize the messenger, but to attend to the message. A woman in the crowd around Jesus once cried out to him, "God bless your mother—the womb from which you came, and the breasts that nursed you!" Surely Mary was greatly blessed to have borne the Son of God. And yet Jesus replied to the woman that there are people even more blessed than she: "all who hear the word of God and put it into practice." (Luke 11:27–28 NLT)

The people of Lystra took Barnabas and Paul to be gods and were about to worship them with garlands and sacrifice. But the apostles ran into the crowd, crying out, "We are merely human beings—just like you! We have come to bring you the Good News that you should turn from these worthless things and turn to the living God, who made heaven and earth, the sea, and everything in them" (Acts 14:15 NLT).

The Book of Hebrews tells us to keep our eyes on Jesus (Heb. 12:2). The angel who spoke to John refused to be worshipped, for the purpose of all prophecy and of all that the angel had shown John was "to tell about Jesus" (Rev. 19:10 NLT). In the city to which we are going, our purpose for being will be ultimately fulfilled when we turn ourselves fully to God and to Christ: "The throne of God and of the Lamb will be there, and his servants will worship him. And they will see his face" (Rev. 22:3–5 NLT).

I cherish my memories of Harold until the time when we can make more. I feel what Albert Kennedy Rowswell expressed in the following poem.

Should You Go First

Should you go first and I remain
to walk the road alone,
I'll live in memory's garden, dear,
with happy days we've known.
In Spring I'll watch for roses red
when fades the lilac blue,
In early Fall when brown leaves fall,
I'll catch a glimpse of you.

Should you go first and I remain
for battles to be fought,
Each thing you've touched along the way
will be a hallowed spot,
I'll hear your voice, I'll see your smile,
though blindly I may grope,

The memory of your helping hand
will bear me on with hope.

Should you go first and I remain
to finish with the scroll,
No length'ning shadows shall creep in
to make this life seem droll.
We've known so much of happiness,
we've had our cup of joy,
And memory is one gift of God,
that death cannot destroy.

Should you go first and I remain,
one thing I'd have you do.
Walk slowly down that long, long path,
for soon I'll follow you.
I'll want to know each step you take,
that I may walk the same,
For some day down that lonely road,
you'll hear me call your name.

I have learned that in order to face God and Christ, we must face ourselves. That is difficult. Nonetheless, the ever-patient God waits as he continues his gentle invitations to us to look to his Word, to freely choose to allow his Spirit to help us, to let his words become alive in our daily experiences. He waits as we plow through defeats and failures until his truth finally sinks down into the depths of our souls—and then we are never the same.

The world is filled with books that were written over the span of thousands of years contemplating what Heaven will be like. Our earthly minds find it difficult to imagine a place with no tears, no pain, no sorrow, no death, people who embody the attributes of Jesus Christ, the light of God's presence, and the many beautiful creations that God alone provides. All of this is wonderful, but to me the most wonderful is to behold the face of God in all of his beauty and to feel the radiance of his love.

In my thoughts I sometimes go back to that scene at sunset by the Etowah River. I faintly hear Harold's voice again, calling me to come to the top of the mountain with him and view the reflection of the sun on the side of the Bridge called Grace.

Although Harold is calling me to come to the place where he is, I know he is not calling me to himself. He is calling me to see the face of God and to enjoy Him for forever.

Afterword

In *God's House! Beautiful! Let's Go!*, Jane Ann Derr has told us more than we have a right to ask. She has let us into the world of her marriage, her family, her work, her loss, her fears, and her happiness. She has let us into her faith in God and her devotion to Jesus Christ. She has let us into her husband's illness and death, and into the grief and resolve of her life as the one who survived.

Jane Ann has striven to tell her story honestly and exactly. If you have tried this yourself, you know how difficult it can be. We like to remember the past better, or worse, than it really was.

We especially like to submerge details in a sea of generalities. But when Jane Ann tells her story, it is concrete and specific. We learn that Harold's '73 Mustang had a 351 Cleveland engine. That she was fired from her job at a car dealership because she could not speak clearly and could not manage the switchboard and was offered another job with the post office as soon as she got home and turned the key in the lock. That Harold grew Leyland cypresses from seedlings that were twelve inches high.

Stories that are specific and particular to the person who tells them help the rest of us to see reality a little clearer. J. R. R. Tolkien understood this, and C. S. Lewis learned it from him. Tolkien said that when a story has the "inner consistency of reality," we catch "a far-off gleam or echo" of God's infinite truth.

The Book of Acts tells us that when Paul reached Jerusalem at the end of his third journey, he and his companions went to see James and the elders of the Jerusalem church. Paul "reported in detail" the events of his work among the Gentiles, and James and the others told of the tens of thousands of Jews who had come to belief in and around Jerusalem. In other words, they told each other their specific and concrete stories. But there was more to it than that. For in telling the stories of their mission to Gentiles and to Jews, they were really telling "what God had done" (Acts 21:19–20).

The same thing often happens as we share our own lives with one another, when we tell our stories carefully and close up. The real interest turns out not to be in ourselves, but in what we have seen of the goodness and mercy of God.

As I have read and reread the things Jane Ann has told in this book, here is what I have seen concerning the common faith of the people of God.

First of all, faith is not merely knowing certain propositions to be true: it is relying on God no matter what seems to be true at the moment. Acting on our faith sometimes seems much more like stepping off the edge of a cliff than like stepping onto solid ground.

This is not the "leap of faith" that we used to hear so much about, in the sense that when we don't know what to believe, we just believe *something*. This is quite different. We already believe the goodness of God and the power of God. But at times we are called upon to act on our faith, without knowing at all what the practical outcome will be. That is the point at which we step off the cliff. In terror and in faith, we step.

We see Jane Ann and Harold stepping off the cliff again and again. And when they do—they find three young couples with forty-six dollars among them. They find a village that will wear the Christian's paper crown. They find the possibility of marriage and children for an enlisted man and his wife in the Air Force. And when Harold steps off the edge of his terminal illness, he finds beauty and a reason for going on.

That is biblical faith—not something for the mind only, but also for the heart and the will, something that emboldens us to take the plunge.

Second, the Bible speaks to us here and now. The Bible is not simply ancient history, a very old book that used to say things to people long ago. It is a book that speaks, as it has always spoken, in the present moment. It spoke a message of hope and judgment to people long ago and drove them forward through fear and change. And it does the same for us. The Bible is a book of both Then and Now.

You can see the Then and Now in the Bible itself: older parts are read and interpreted in newer parts. The prophet Daniel "understood from the Scriptures" that Jeremiah had spoken of seventy years of exile, and finds a further meaning for the captive people of God in seventy weeks of years (Dan. 9). Paul read of Moses and the cloud and the sea, and concluded that baptized, communing church members, too, can be overthrown in the wilderness (1 Cor. 10). The author of Hebrews was a great scholar of the written text; but for him the text was not a dry and a dead thing: it was something "alive and active" unleashed on us to bring us bare into the light of God's presence, "today, when you hear his voice" (Heb. 4:12–13; 3:7).

When Helene asks on the porch swing, "Do you think that God will take care of you now?" it is not only a question for Jane Ann. It is a question for all of us. There are times when it seems glib and insincere for us to beam and say, "Of course he will." Too much is at stake, and we are pressed down by too much sorrow and heartache for glib answers. In such times, a word spoken ages ago to others means little to us. What we must have is a present word spoken to *us*. The words of Paul to Timothy become that word for us: "God has not given us a spirit of fear, but of power and of love and of a sound mind."

Third, prayer is not our last recourse, but our first. Of course God hears the prayer we say in the last split second before we hit the ground. But if we aim at Paul's idea to "pray without ceasing," we will not wait that long. In fact, things will begin in prayer, not merely end.

That is all standard fare and we have heard it a thousand times. We have less often seen what it looks like in practice. That is why it is good for us to read of Harold's constant summons, "Let's pray about it," to read of nightly prayers for discernment, to read that Janice and Jane Ann said a prayer and *then* got into the car and headed out to help. We see prayer that is as much a part of life as breathing.

Viewed in one way prayers are as transient as the breaths that utter them. We breathe our prayer and move on. Mankind breathes its million prayers and moves on. Yet viewed in another way, prayers are as enduring as the God who hears them. He attends to our prayers, takes them into account, and disposes the universe accordingly. The presence of our prayers is one of the things that makes the universe what it is.

It can therefore be a good spiritual exercise to keep our prayers in a journal. We can come back to them years later and learn something about God and how he has responded, and about ourselves and how we have changed. Jane Ann has done that, and she opens her journals to us in this book. To take one example, she has given us an entry from 1965 that describes God's provision in a difficult time (this is at the end of Chapter 5). Beyond describing a past experience, the journal entry reaches forward to her forty years later and gives her resolve for that difficult time, too. In the writing of this book, she has drawn on her journals, written before the memories faded, and they serve to encourage us as well.

One of prayer's puzzles is that we address them to an all-knowing God who already knows what is in them. The question that arises from this is, "Why pray them?" As a philosophical question, it invites thought (and we might, for example, answer that such prayer is, on our end, a means of maintaining a relationship with God).

But as a practical question, it hardly makes any difference at all. In our prayers we constantly remind

God of who he is and what he is supposed to know. It sounds odd to say it, for of course God does not need to be reminded who he is and what he knows. And yet if you look at what people actually say in prayer, you find that they do an awful lot of reminding. Five minutes with a concordance has turned up the following examples. Moses: "Remember your servants Abraham, Isaac and Jacob. Overlook the stubbornness of this people" (Deut. 9:27). Samson: "Sovereign Lord, remember me. Please, God, strengthen me just once more" (Judg. 16:28). Hezekiah: "Remember, Lord, how I have walked before you faithfully and with wholehearted devotion" (2 Kings 20:3). Nehemiah: "Remember me for this also, my God, and show mercy to me according to your great love" (Neh. 13:22). Job: "Remember that you molded me like clay. Will you now turn me to dust again?" (Job 10:9). A psalmist: "Remember your word to your servant, for you have given me hope" (Ps. 119:49). Habakkuk: "In wrath remember mercy" (Hab. 3:2). And here is only one modern example, from the prayer book of the Church of Ireland: "Remember for good all those that love us, and those that hate us and those that have desired us, unworthy as we are, to pray for them. And those whom we have forgotten, do thou, O Lord, remember."

There is much that we want God to remember, for there is much that he has promised: to be with us always, even to the end of the age; to listen to what we say to him and to take notice of our prayers; to fill us with his love and his spirit; to look upon us in

Christ as if we had never sinned; that we will not be tested beyond what we can bear; that the powers of evil will never defeat the power of good. These are the promises we hold on to, and they get us through most days.

But then there are days when our burdens seem to pile up. We discover that people are flawed and imperfect, and that the world is not always safe and welcoming. We discover that we, too, are flawed and are not as virtuous and wise as we thought. We discover that the beauty and vigor we once had will eventually wane, that life does not last forever. Add to this life's accidents and misfortunes—illness, disappointment, seeming failures, breakdown of friendships—there is no point in naming them all— and days will come when God seems to have forgotten us.

Those are the days when in weakness and fear we are liable to remind God of who he is and what he is supposed to know. "God! Remember! You promised! Never more than we can bear! Never to forsake us! Always to love us and to be at our side in the night!"

When we pray in this way, we will find God to be as good as his word. His anger will melt into love. Through loss and pain will come growth and wisdom and joy. We will find that no matter what happens, when we have the love of God and the grace of God, we have enough. We will find that in all phases of life, God is the highest good and the deepest desire. We will find it the greatest blessing of all to know God and to know the love of God.

Prayer like that is not a last recourse, a desperation measure when all else has failed. It is a way of naming our deepest hopes about God. And as soon as we name them, we find the ground under us again. Prayer, by putting the firm ground of God's mercies under our feet, is the first step in taking the next step into life with God.

Fourth, the purposes of God and the promises of God are not defeated by calamity or death or anything else.

Granted, the power of death appears complete. Anyone who has seen it knows that death is deadly. Anyone who dares think of it knows that all things eventually succumb to it. The grave never says, "Enough."

It is only an opinion of mine, but it looks to me as if things die because they do not have inherent in themselves and of themselves the power not to, and once dead, do not have in themselves and of themselves the power to live again. If this supposition is true, the ancient question, "If a man die, shall he live again?" (Job 14:14 KJV) has only one answer: "If the Lord wills."

Now it is not my opinion only, but it is the message at the heart and center of the gospel that Jesus died and lives, and that this is in accord with the will of God. The hope of the gospel is that one day the story of dying and rising will be our own story as well, and that this, too, is in accord with the will of God.

Therefore we soldier on to the end, not because we can overcome, but because we hope in the God who has overcome. And we do not give up hope, for our soldiering is not in vain. In the resurrection all of our history, all of our pain, sorrow, and yearning, will be brought into the presence of God and transformed: weakness into strength, corruption into incorruption, death into life, sorrow into joy.

Our present labor therefore has meaning and value, for in the resurrection God will gather us up from death into his presence, which is life. Nothing will have been lost, nothing will have gone for naught, nothing will have been in vain. Our strivings and sufferings will in Christ be given validation and meaning, for our entire histories, even our bowing to death, will bring us into the presence of God.

This Harold understood, along with generations of believers, and this is the glimpse into the eternal reality of God embodied in the title of this book and written into every page.

Stephen Broyles

A missionary venture to Ghana
during turbulent times. Learn
to walk on water.

Trailblazing with God is author Jane Ann
Derr's account of how she and her husband
Harold went to Ghana, West Africa, with their
five children in the early 1960s, a time of
political upheaval in Africa as well as America.

Trailblazing with God by Jane Ann Derr
Xulon Press
ISBN 978-1-60477-866-3
Order from the author at
godshousebeautiful@yahoo.com
Also in bookstores and online and availabe for
download on most eReader platforms.

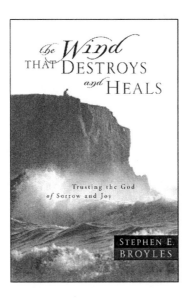

LaVergne, TN USA
26 February 2011
217986LV00003B/2/P

9 781612 157993